Writing With Style

The news story and the feature

by Peter Jacobi

Lawrence Ragan Communications, Inc.   Chicago

ISBN 0-931368-12-X

Published by
Lawrence Ragan Communications, Inc.
407 S. Dearborn Street
Chicago, IL 60605

Introduction

It's so easy to become a drudge, a drone, even as a writer.

Particularly as a writer.

To become listless. To lose one's tenacity.

I recall it as a student, as a reporter, as a network newsman, as a magazine editor, as a critic and freelancer, as editor of student papers, as job holder, as consultant.

The promise of a task soon changes to pattern. The excitement transforms into tedium.

As perhaps you feel. As most likely you feel. "Oh, no, not another speech to cover," you'll tell yourself. "Oh, no, not another retirement story." Not another laboratory opening. Not another plant closing. Not another new product announcement. Not another quarterly earnings report. Not another holiday schedule. Not another conference. Not another benefits package. Not another economic roundup. Not another academic survey. Not another dreary assignment. "Lord, help me get through it."

I think my turn-around from apathy and lethargy came while reading two paragraphs from a speech the great Justice Oliver Wendell Holmes gave to the Harvard Law School Association of New York in February of 1913. He was not a professional writer. He was a professional thinker. But in that speech he had something to say, and he took the time to consider how to say it. From his care and in his accomplishment flowered a lesson for me. I think in what he wrote there may be a lesson for all of us who write:

> If I am right, it will be a slow business for our people to reach rational views, assuming that we are allowed to work peaceably to that end. But as I grow older, I grow calm. If I feel what are perhaps an old man's apprehensions, that competition from new races will cut deeper than working men's disputes and will test whether we can hang together and can fight; if I fear that we are running through the world's resources at a pace that we cannot keep; I do not lose my hopes. I do not pin my dreams for the future to my country or even to my race. I think it probable that civilizations somehow will last as long as I care to look ahead—perhaps with smaller numbers, but perhaps also bred to greatness and splendor by science. I think it not improbable that man. . .may have cosmic destinies that he does not understand. And so beyond the vision of battling races and an impoverished earth, I catch a dreaming glimpse of peace.

> The other day my dream was pictured to my mind. It was evening. I was walking homeward on Pennsylvania Avenue near the Treasury, and as I looked beyond Sherman's statue to the west, the sky was aflame with scarlet and crimson from the setting sun. But, like the note of downfall in Wagner's opera, below the sky line there came from little globes the pallid discord of the electric lights. And I thought to myself the *Gotterdammerung* will end, and from those globes clustered like evil eggs will come the new masters of the sky. It is like the time in which we live. But then I remembered the faith that I partly have expressed, faith in a universe not measured by our fears, a universe that has thought and more than thought inside of it, and as I gazed, after the sunset and above the electric lights, there shone the stars.

Holmes did not know of World Wars I and II nor of a civil rights movement nor of a Third World nor of warplanes nor of Nazis nor of environmental concerns nor of energy shortages. But all these have come to pass. And since the stars still shine, perhaps we'll somehow get from here to there.

What a piece of writing: its phraseology and its meaning.

Whenever I get dumpy, I think about Justice Holmes and the stars that keep on shining. And suddenly I realize how fortunate I am to write for a living. Tough as it is.

It is my opportunity and challenge, after all, to set in words, to explain, to describe a tickle, a scratch, an itch. . .the perception of a rose upon the nostrils and the touch of a raindrop on the skin. . .a kiss and satisfaction. . .the caress of tongue by meat and soup. . .the heaven's blue. . . the feathery softness of a bed and the steel of steel. . .the sting of an ant. . .the sensation of a cough and a sneeze. . .sand sifting through fingers. . .the many sounds of music. . .a howling child and a laughing one. . .a fire. . .a hand parting hair. . .a cat lapping milk and the animal's purr. . .leaves flying along roads of wind. . .walking barefoot through mud. . .a cloud and a mountain. . .snow. . .red and white. . .a waterfall. . .the face of a child and ice cream. . .the crack of a ball against a bat. . .the whirr of a machine. . .salt and pepper. . .an egg shell smashed against the side of a dish. . .a skin's wrinkle. . .a wave upon the sea. . .a field of wheat. . .the pungency of hay and alfalfa. . . the eyes of a woman and the expression of her figure. . .the eyes of a man and the expression of his. . .a word upon paper. . .a painting and the feel of brush strokes on canvas. . .smoke and ashes. . .glass. . .the power of air in the lungs. . .the smoothness of silk. . .the sparkle of an emerald. . .the tick-tock of a clock. . .the dizzy contentment of wine. . .flowers and velvet. . .a heartbeat.

All this is the world of non-fiction. All this is the world of a writer.

We can learn from the painter. Rouault, speaking of his work, once said: "In truth, I have painted by opening my eyes day and night on the perceptible world, and also by closing them from time to time that I might better see the vision blossom and submit itself to orderly arrangement." It is what we, as writers, need to do.

That disturbing yet always truth-seeking author, Henry Miller, acknowledged that a writer "has antennae" and "knows how to hook up to the currents which are in the atmosphere, in the cosmos; he merely has the facility for hooking on, as it were. Who is original? Everything that we are doing, everything that we think, exists already, and we are only intermediaries, that's all, who make use of what is in the air."

It's rather wonderful to "make use of what is in the air," far better than looking down at the dirty sidewalk.

John Ciardi, when he served as poetry editor for *Saturday Review,* noted that the writer is "overpowered by words, sentences, rhythms, ideas, the drama of ideas when there are lives moving in them, and the forms he can shape from his medium. Language haunts him. Words, sentences, rhythms are not things to him; they are presences. . . .His medium is a gorgeous confusion upon him and a gorgeous flowering of all possibility. It is his house of great ghosts."

You have no right to get fed up with your work when all that's within your constant grasp. And even when the assignment seems purest drudgery, remember what the cultural philosopher Erwin Edman said: "Experience is full of dead spots. Art gives it life." Through your handling of an event or your observation of a person, you can cut out the dead spots—edit them out—and give a sense of heightened life to what you have experienced and what your readers now will experience through you.

What a lovely thing to do for others.

I remember a television talk show host once telling me that from each expert he invites on his show he attempts to elicit the details of his or her everyday experience. "It is humdrum to the experts, but the expert's humdrum is fresh and new and exciting for the rest of us." That's what a good writer also attempts to do. Holmes did it. Rouault focused on it. Miller said we have antennae to do it. Ciardi told us to be overpowered by it. Edman explained its meaning.

May this book help you to remember that you write, and that to write can mean you touch the stars. May this book always instruct and at least sometimes inspire.

It does less and it does more

Two recent articles I chanced across emphasize the limits and the powers of writing.

Jan Hoffman, in a review of several travel books for *The Village Voice,* says:

> Why travel? my friend the querulous xenophobe asked recently. What's the point? You've seen photographs of the Eiffel Tower taken from every position imaginable. The Khmer Rouge Ballet travels to *us.* There isn't a place left on the globe that hasn't been picked over and written about by anthropologists, sociologists, journalists, or memoirists. Explain what possible enjoyment you derive from spending 20 sleepless hours on an overcrowded train, just to get to some spot you could read about in the comfort of your own home.

> I fired off many explanations, all of which amounted to one of the oldest tantrums in the world: "Because I want to see for myself."

> Travelers are Doubting Thomases: they truculently hold guides and accounts suspect until they can confirm them with first-hand experience. But it is true that the most vivid reports back can only give approximations of a place. Once, I got off a local Italian bus, feeling a victim of the worst tourist impulses, and abruptly burst out laughing: nothing I'd read prepared me for the first jolt—the Leaning Tower of Pisa looked *ludicrous.* Being in the place itself gives a sharp immediacy of sensation, the overwhelming headiness of context.

There are limits to writing. Certainly an observing writer, and a powerful one, can through his or her words do much to recreate a scene or an event. Narration and description can bring the reader very close. But writing is, after all, a recreation or a verbal approximation of the real thing.

The writer faces that problem always and forever. It's what gives him emotional hives but also keeps him striving to do better.

And in the striving the writer sometimes discovers that words can give a unique power to a scene or event or thing. I mentioned that I'd read two articles. The other was in "The Talk of the Town" column of the *New Yorker,* in which a woman correspondent writes of sitting on a very cold winter day with a friend who had her first child just two days earlier and who was at that point nursing it. They talk in a fifth floor loft. This is the paragraph that grabbed hold of me:

> Frost spreads on the windows, and in the freezing sunlight out on Twentieth Street men wearing Air Force jackets and leather hats with earflaps are unloading a truck; up the street, men are hauling bed frames for a wholesale furniture place near the corner, backing cars out of a garage, or hanging out in the J & D Restaurant (*comidas, hamburguesas*). Now National Public Radio has begun the Prelude to *Parsifal,* and I am struck by the different types of time I can observe, sitting where I am: there are the ambitious, doom-laden rhythms of the music; there is the day of the men in the street, which is measured in eight-hour or ten-hour shifts, coffee breaks, and muscles contracting in the cold; there is the beat I can't hear in the dance studio directly across from where we sit, to which the dancers (turned into brownish silhouettes by sheets of plastic tacked over the windows against the winter) are performing brisk rondes de jambes en l'air; there is the desultory pace of the mysterious business on the floor above the dance studio, where a young man lounges for hours in front of a telephone in an office from whose rafters hang net bags full of round dark objects (bowler hats? baskets? coconuts?); and there is the cocoon in which this mother and baby are at present existing, a dimension in which minutes can pass like years, and the conventional divisions of the day—work time, leisure; darkness, light—are dissolved in the face of a passionate mutual absorption that eclipses the rest of the world.

Not only was I interested in the paragraph because what's described took place within two blocks of my own Manhattan home, but because the author has revealed so clearly what writing *can* do that real-life can*not.* She has given us five kinds of time, all happening at once, and with her words compressed, contrasted, and juxtaposed them. Her powers of observation and her contextual use of words have combined to heighten a scene, to make it more than it would seem to be.

The writer faces this potential always and forever. It's what gives him the push to the typewriter.

The writer can highlight a moment or moments, as above, or fact:

Seventeen million children around the world died from hunger or disease in 1981, according to the annual report of the United Nations Children's Fund. Unicef said the deaths could have been prevented at the cost of under $100 for each child.

"Far from being priceless, a child's life was worth less than $100 in 1981," James P. Grant, the fund's executive director, wrote in a report.

The writer can magnify a feeling, as does Maureen Crockett in a "Seems to Me" guest column for American Airlines' *American Way*:

One of the most pleasant aspects of flying is that the phone doesn't ring. Ownership of a phone, to paraphrase William Faulkner, puts me at the mercy of any damn fool with a dime and a finger to dial with.

As a landscape artist I am working at home most of the day, and I get some weird calls. A ringing phone is importunate. It might be my husband calling to say, "Let me take you out to that new expensive restaurant tonight." It might be President Reagan wanting my input on the tax cut. It might be the bank saying, "We made a mistake in your checking account. Add $100 to your checkbook." What it is is some company wanting to photograph my family cheap.

Sometimes I get heavy breathers. When I was young, such calls terrified me. Now they are fun. I breathe heavily right back, then both of us, hyperventilated, hang up.

The writer can stop time, freeze-frame action and emotions as Norman Mailer does in his non-fictional fiction, or is it fictional non-fiction, *The Armies of the Night*, his version of the 1967 march on the Pentagon by anti-Vietnam war activists.

It was not unlike being a boy about to jump from one garage roof to an adjoining garage roof. The one thing not to do was wait. Mailer looked at Macdonald and Lowell. "Let's go," he said. Not looking again at them, not pausing to gather or dissipate resolve, he made a point of stepping neatly and decisively over the low rope. Then he headed across the grass to the nearest MP he saw.

It was as if the air had changed, or light had altered; he felt immediately much more alive—yes, bathed in air—and yet disembodied from himself, as if indeed he were watching himself in a film where this action was taking place. He could feel the eyes of the people behind the rope watching him, could feel the intensity of their existence as spectators. And as he walked forward, he and the MP looked at one another with the naked stricken lucidity which comes when absolute strangers are for the moment absolutely locked together.

The MP lifted his club to his chest as if to bar all passage. To Mailer's great surprise—he had secretly expected the enemy to be calm and strong, why should they not? they had every power, all the guns—to his great surprise, the MP was trembling. He was a young Negro, part white, who looked to have come from some small town where perhaps there were not many other Negroes; he had at any rate no Harlem smoke, no devil swish, no black, no black power for him, just a simple boy in an Army suit with a look of horror in his eye. "Why, why did it have to happen to me?" was the message of the petrified marbles in his face.

"Go back," he said hoarsely to Mailer.

Notice how simple much of the above is. But the words have been carefully selected and the cadences just as carefully measured. Careful creativity can result in writing that circumvents limits and reaches bigger-than-life dimensions.

And meanwhile, *in* Vietnam, according to Jimmy Breslin:

George Sunderland rolled over on his cot in the hut and his foot caught the mosquito netting and pulled part of it onto the bed. Mosquito netting should hang straight, from the rod on the ceiling over the cot down to the floor, so that the rat crawling up it follows the netting to the ceiling and does not get a grip on the cot with its feet. Sunderland's foot made a fold in the netting and the rat crawling up it came into the fold and onto the bed. The rat's small mouth moved and its teeth came through the netting and into Sunderland's foot. Sunderland kicked the rat and the rat fell under the cot. The rat crept away with its tail dragging across the dirt floor.

George Sunderland, who is a sergeant in the Special Forces, had to be taken out of his camp at a place called Plateau GI the next morning. The doctors started treating him for rabies by sticking aluminum needles into his stomach.

Vietnam, which is a little war of rats, is like this always. It is a place of sneaking and gnawing and of people who see nothing and hear nothing and spend days finding nothing, and who are hit in the back by a shot that comes from nowhere. Nothing seems to happen, and then a Marine battalion is sent home after seven months and it has not been in one action and it has 10 per cent casualties.

Breslin transports us through time and space. Even today that happening seems as now. Even from our office or living room as we read the report it seems as here.

The writer also can make a small event grow in import and even into symbol. Take Theodore White's account of a telethon during the West Virginia primary of 1960. Hubert Humphrey sits in a TV studio answering the questions of callers-in.

The first question was a normal mechanical question: "What makes you think you're qualified to be President, Senator Humphrey?" So was the second question: "Can you be nominated, Mr. Humphrey?"

Then came a rasping voice over the telephone, the whining scratch of an elderly lady somewhere high in the hills, and one could see Humphrey flinch (as the viewers flinched); and the rasp said, "You git out! You git out of West Virginia, Mr. Humphrey!" Humphrey attempted to fluster a reply and the voice overrode him, "You git out, you hear! You can't stand the Republicans gitting ahead of you! Why don't you git out?"

Humphrey had barely recovered from the blast before the next call came: what would he do about small-arms licensing for people who like to hunt? Then, what would he do about social security? None of the questions were hitting anywhere near the target area of Humphrey's campaign program, and then a sweet womanly voice began to drawl on the open switch, "How about those poor little neglected children, Mr. Humphrey, I mean how can we lower taxes like you say and take care of all those little children who need more schools and more hospitals, and more everything. . ." On and on she went, sweetly, as Humphrey (his precious, costly minutes oozing by) attempted to break in and say that he, too, was for the poor little neglected children.

By now the telethon was becoming quite a family affair, and the next voice was a fine mountain voice, easy, slow, gentle with West Virginia courtesy, and it said, "Senator Humphrey, I just want you to know that I want to apologize for that lady who told you to git out. We don't feel like that down here in West Virginia, Senator Humphrey, and I'm very sorry that she said that. . . ." He would have rambled on and on, but Humphrey, desperate, expressed quick thanks and pressed the other button.

And on, ever worse. To White the event reveals the unpromising, almost hopeless nature of the Humphrey campaign. It also obviously is a symbol of the lunacy to which an election campaign can descend.

Maybe there are limits to writing, but think of all you *can* do. To make such wonders happen is your opportunity and challenge. That's not a bad way to make a living.

The agony and the ecstasy: writing on the job

Maybe you've seen a variation of the "only" game somewhere or other. Writing instructors use it in classes to show how moving a single word within a sentence can alter meaning drastically. "Only I love you." "I love you only." There's a world of difference between the two.

And sometimes when we're not careful, we create not merely a changed meaning but an absurdity, as in this caption to a photograph: "This is part of a silver coffee service supported by replicas of chicken legs which belonged to Mrs. Abraham Lincoln."

Over the years, educators and business people alike have addressed the problem of writing language. From writing proficiency tests to required composition courses in schools and industry, various approaches have been tried to cure the ills of bad writing.

Unfortunately, the problems persist. There's so much bad writing in business because there's so much bad writing everywhere. Another reason why the writing malady continues to ail businesses is that too many business people don't consider writing a primary responsibility.

But today, writing has become a major responsibility, one with which even chief executive officers have to deal. A successful business, more than ever, depends on satisfying the public, its customers. Public satisfaction depends on how the public is served. Service has come to depend, at least partially, on communication, explanation, information or, basically, on words.

Every letter, every memo, every report, every appearance, every speech is an opportunity and an obligation, an opportunity for communication and, therefore, an obligation for the communicator, you, to be as clear and as communicative as you can be. Unless you manage to get your message across, what good is your writing? Be it an informal memo to your boss, an announcement posted on a bulletin board, a letter to another organization, a message to a customer or a project proposal, if your writing doesn't convey your thoughts accurately, completely and clearly, you haven't gotten your message across.

Often, when you communicate, you seek response. That means you seek to persuade: persuade your boss to accept a plan; persuade a client to accept your company's services; persuade secretaries to adopt a new office technique; persuade a public to listen.

Persuasion is not easy. It gets more difficult all the time. So the more weapons you have in your communications arsenal, the more likely it is you can meet the problems of a situation and persuade your readers or listeners to respond.

Unfortunately, many people in business lose sight of their purpose when they write. They sacrifice their message and mission to persuade for businessese, a dialect of our language that contains the longest words available strung together to form sentences so lengthy that the reader has to take a coffee break in the middle.

Writing in business is not an opportunity to show off writing skills. You seek primarily to express your thoughts so that your reader or listener can understand them. You also want people to pay attention because without understanding and a certain amount of interest or enthusiasm, you're not likely to get action.

Maybe it's true that "when two or more operative procedures are performed in different operative incisions, we pay the amount listed in the schedule of allowances for the procedure which has the greater allowance and one half of the amount listed in the schedule of allowances for the procedure(s) with the lesser amount." But for the customer of that insurance company, understanding would have been more likely if the message read: "When a patient undergoes two or more related operations, the insurance company pays the full allowance scheduled for the most expensive surgery and one half for the others."

As important and essential as the three Rs—reading, 'riting and 'rithmetic—are in education, that's how important and essential the 10 Cs are in writing. Whenever you put pen to paper, you should be:

- clear
- concise
- complete
- constructive
- credible
- correct
- coherent
- conversational
- captivating
- considerate

To be *clear:*
(1) Know what your message is.
(2) Organize. Make an outline that contains major points.
(3) Use simple sentences.
(4) Beware of jargon.
(5) Avoid "I have status" words such as optimize and cognize and dichotomize, paradigm and matrix.
(6) Use the active voice. Don't say: "A test of readership was made by following what those in the survey group read and did not read in each day's newspaper." Make it: "We tested readership habits by determining what stories people read or ignored in each day's newspaper."
(7) Use simple, familiar words. (Choose fire over conflagration; repeat instead of reiterate.)

To be *concise,* be careful. Edit your work. Why say: "I am sincerely pleased" when "I am pleased" means the same thing? Don't say: "Mr. Clark will be responsible for the development of all new salespeople and the supervision of these people as well as others who are on our sales force." Instead, write: "Mr. Clark will develop all new salespeople and supervise our sales force."

In other words, to be concise, reduce the language. Write what you want to say, and be done with it. You've no right to waste anyone's time. Besides, the more words, the more likely that some readers will get confused.

To be *complete,* put yourself into the reader's (or listener's) mind, and determine what he or she would want or need to know and answer those questions. Don't try to include too much. It's better to make one point well than to introduce 15 and leave your reader perplexed.

To be *constructive,* consider tone and your method of approach. "It's been a lousy year," says the chief executive officer. "We should all be ashamed of ourselves. Business is rotten. Sales levels are scandalous." Well, no wonder. He might have said: "Even though we had hoped for a better year, we made great progress in certain areas. And I see signs that point to an upsurge in at least three of those where we had losses. Now, I think we can team up to. . ."

Why be negative by saying: "Your letter is not clear. I don't understand your question." Better to write: "Before I can answer your question, I need more information. Please explain. . ."

To be *credible,* know your audience and consider what they are likely to accept from you. Also, provide the type of information and use an approach appropriate to the occasion. Support your views by using authorities respected by your audience.

A description of the company's newest computer system, for example, could contain highly technical terms if the report will be read by engineers, systems analysts or programmers. But if you plan to distribute the report to all employees, some of whom have no technical background, use language that everyone will understand.

To be *correct,* check and double check your information. People may make decisions based on the information you present.

To be *coherent,* sort things out in your own mind so you can share the information logically with your audience. Is this paragraph logical?

AIR, Assistance for Interested Retirees, was founded 15 years ago. Now its membership includes 250 of the nation's largest corporations. It began when 25 corporations collaborated to create programs of work and help for senior citizens. It's estimated that about 4,000 firms belong to local councils affiliated with the national organization. The organization's reason for being is to help senior citizens cope with the economy and personal economics.

The information does not flow logically. Let's re-order.

AIR, Assistance for Interested Retirees, was founded 15 years ago. The organization's reason for being is to help senior citizens cope with the economy and personal economics. It began when 25 corporations collaborated to create programs of work and help for senior citizens. Now its membership includes 250 of the nation's largest corporations. It's estimated that about 4,000 firms belong to local councils affiliated with the national organization.

To be *conversational,* read your copy out loud. Listen to your writing. Let the ears catch what the eyes tend to miss. If what you've put to paper sounds stiff and formal, unlike you, then think again about how better to express your sentiments or statistics. By listening to what you write, you'll improve not only that piece of writing but all your writing.

Does the following sound conversational?

In regard to the subject account mentioned above, please find the enclosed statement. . .

A human being would say:

You wrote of a problem about the account. Here's the breakdown. . .

To be *captivating:*
(1) Think of what gets your attention.
(2) If others shout, you whisper; be different.
(3) Humanize your material.

Writer Freya Stark some years ago recalled arriving for the first time in Cairo. She was appalled by the poverty, by the throngs of beggars. Yet even her emotions cooled in the droning chorus of "Alms for the love of Allah." Amidst that chorus, one beggar approached Freya Stark, looked into her face, and said, "By God, I am hungry." And she heard.

To be *considerate,* don't try people's patience. Get to the point.

What you write or say first is important, perhaps most important. That first statement— the lead—serves to establish the subject, set the tone, attract attention, and guide into the material that follows.

That's why "In the beginning God created the heaven and the earth" is so good.

On its own level so is: "We like your idea. Consider yourself hired."

But from the lead to the last sentence, remember your purpose: to communicate a message and persuade the reader to respond. If what you write is a burden for you to read, or boring or confusing, then readers will see it that way, too.

When you sit down to write, think of yourself at the reading or listening end. What keeps you alert? What puts you to sleep? Make your words work for you. Aim your writing at readers, not

into a vacuum. That's harder, no doubt. But you'll write better that way.

And, oh, how we need better writing.

QUIZ

Here's a short quiz to test your writing skills. Something is wrong with each of the sentences below. Some contain errors in grammar and punctuation; others violate one or more of the "10 Cs." Rules for correct usage and ways to improve these sentences follow. If you can't recognize any of the problems and don't know where to begin, start by getting hold of a good grammar text or stylebook.

A mix of problems
1. It is the intention of the manager to provide an evaluation as to the performance of John Doe in the modernization of the company's plant.
2. It tastes good like a cigarette should.
3. The new radio telescope can be compared with a giant ear, and has an infinite range compared to the earlier model.
4. Hopefully, morale will improve in the office.
5. Macy's is having a storewide clearance sale. They are offering almost every item at a discount.
6. Because of illness neither the president nor the vice president were able to attend.
7. You will take the 6:30 a.m. flight to North Carolina. Then you will meet the plant's manager. Then you will tour the plant. Then you will write a report.
8. The fact is we are not meeting our objectives.
9. My first job with the company will always be remembered.
10. These 12 persons comprise the purchasing department.

Some solutions and rules
1. This statement ignores an important "C," concise, and is an example of businessese. More simply stated: "The manager will evaluate how well John Doe modernizes the plant."
2. The "as/like" rule. "Like" usually governs nouns and pronouns; "as" is used before clauses and phrases that contain verbs. It

tastes good as a cigarette should.

3. Compared *to* assumes basic similarity. Compared *with* contrasts dissimilar qualities. So, the sentence should read: "The new radio telescope can be compared to a giant ear, and has an infinite range compared with the earlier model."

4. Hopefully means "'with hope," not "I hope" or "it is to be hoped." Correctly used: "I hope morale will improve in the office."

5. Macy's is a collective noun that takes a singular verb. The first sentence is correct; the second should be: "It is offering almost every item at a discount."

6. If neither/nor (and either/or) link singular nouns, the verb in the sentence should be singular: "Because of illness neither the president nor the vice president was able to attend."

7. Strive for variety of sentence structure. How about: "Take the 6:30 a.m. flight to North Carolina to meet with the plant's manager. Then tour the plant. When you return, please write a report."

8. If it is a fact, just state it in a straightforward manner: "We are not meeting our objectives."

9. Use the active voice: "I will always remember my first job with the company."

10. The whole comprises its parts; the parts constitute the whole: "The purchasing department comprises these 12 persons."

Read to write

Know what's important to you if you're a writer or editor?

Reading.

I don't mean just your manuscript and those of others. That just goes with the territory. I don't mean just the literature of your profession. That also just goes with the territory.

I mean you should really read.

Literature. Magazines. Newspapers. New books and old. And read not only for information but with eyes and heart and mind open to style, to writing techniques.

How much you can learn. Another writer, in a completely different genre or situation, may have solved a writing problem whose solution has eluded you. Or he may open your eyes to methods of construction, of approach, of ways to use the language which release your work from temporary or long-shackled bonds.

Examples? They're everywhere. In recent days I've been enriched (something that never fails to happen whenever I permit myself the time to catch up on reading).

Take this contrast lead of then and now, about a figure out of memory who's still very much around and wants to remind us he is. It's from the *New York Times*: author, Steven Roberts:

> He ran for President once. The television crews came around, then, and the police escorts and the cheering crowds.
>
> Then he lost. The scent of power vanished as fast as it had come. And now, eight years later, he was back home, walking the streets and shaking the hands and making the small talk, practically alone, a figure out of history trying to win one more chunk of the future.
>
> Senator George McGovern is running hard for re-election, very hard. . . .

Well crafted. Evocative.

As are the lines in Jack Krol's review for *Newsweek* of "Ordinary People," the Robert Redford-directed smash. He speaks of the performance given by a well-known personality Krol obviously thought didn't have it in her:

> . . .he [Redford] saw something in TV's Mary Tyler Moore that nobody else saw—the tension behind that all-American smile. In Beth that

smile, stretching Moore's mouth and neck tendons in a flying buttress of rigid control, becomes scary.

Krol says much in a few words. As does Lewis Grossberger in his capsules about programs for the new TV season in *New York* magazine, as when he writes, " 'Hill Street Blues'. . .can only be either great or awful, and you know where the odds point." And when he says, "Despite all our efforts to stop him, Danny Thomas is back on TV in 'But I'm a Big Girl Now.'. . .A new generation is about to learn the true meaning of the word 'sickening.' "

Or take John J. O'Connor's comment, " 'Shogun'. . .may be the world's costliest language lesson," in his *New York Times* piece about that program.

What was it advertising man Hal Stebbins said? "Bring me the sunset in a cup."

Good writers, such as these, do it all the time.

I was impressed also with Thomas Moore's handling in the *Chicago Sun-Times* of the prestidigitation that always goes on concerning our national budget. You know, "We'll get rid of the deficit," says the politician, and then "we" never do. Moore explains why. "More than one-quarter of the federal budget goes to the elderly, most of it as Social Security benefits and Medicare. . . .Another quarter of the budget goes for national defense. . . .Approximately 11 percent of federal spending is interest on the national debt, which is approaching $1 trillion. . . .With so much of the federal budget taken by these three items, any significant reduction in spending would take an enormous bite out of the remaining programs." He explains that a ten per cent spending cut exempting the above untouchables "would require cutting all other federal programs by 25 per cent. That would mean, among other things, cutting by one-quarter the budgets for the FBI, highway construction, food stamps, and care for disabled veterans." Result: dilemma. I suddenly understand.

Moore has used statistics well. They illuminate.

A deft bit of description comes from Roger Angell in his beautiful profile for the *New Yorker* of my favorite (and my younger son's favorite) baseball figure, St. Louis pitching legend Bob Gibson. Angell writes:

> Although he was of only moderate size for a pitcher—six feet one and about a hundred and eighty-five pounds—Gibson always appeared to take up a lot of space on the mound, and the sense of intimidation. . .had something to do with his sombre, almost funereal demeanor as he stared in at his catcher, with his cap pulled low over his black face and strong jaw, and with the ball held behind his right hip (he always wore a sweatshirt under his uniform, with the long, Cardinals-red sleeves extending all the way down to his wrists), and with his glove cocked on his left hip, parallel to the ground. Everything about him looked mean and loose—arms, elbows, shoulders, even his legs—as, with a quick little shrug, he launched into his delivery.

And what did I say about learning from literature? Yes, from fiction, such as "The Swan," which I chanced across again on a flight from Chicago to St. Louis in the Ozark Airlines magazine, of all places. The story comes from Ray Bradbury's *Dandelion Wine.* It's about the lovely relationship of a 31-year-old man and a remarkable nonagenarian who shared with him her life and travels, and who at one point explains to him what it's like to be as she is, old.

The young man when younger had seen a picture of her as a debutante. "So you think I was pretty?" she asks.

He nodded good-humoredly.

> "But how can you tell?" she asked. "When you meet a dragon that has eaten a swan, do you guess by the few feathers around the mouth? That's what it is—a body like this is a dragon, all scales and folds. So the dragon ate the white swan. I haven't seen her for years. I can't even remember what she looks like, I *feel* her, though. She's safe inside, still alive: the essential swan hasn't changed a feather. Do you know, there are some mornings in spring or fall, when I wake and think, I'll run across the fields into the woods and pick wild strawberries! Or I'll swim in the lake, or I'll dance all night tonight until dawn! And, then, in a rage, discover I'm in this old and ruined dragon. I'm the princess in the crumbled tower, no way out, waiting for her Prince Charming.

Has there ever been a better definition of aging? I wept. Bradbury has captured in a nugget feelings deeply felt.

That's what one gets from reading encourage you to go on your own treasure hunt (and with regularity).

The Pulitzer story—reading writing

I urge you to read.

Read to write. Read to write better.

"I will cry a hundred years from now, no matter how many memories come and go," wrote Rich Heiland in the Xenia (Ohio) *Gazette,* "when I think of what this wind did to my city and its people."

Heiland and the *Gazette* won a Pulitzer Prize for Local General Reporting in 1975. His story about a killer tornado is included in *The Pulitzer Prize Story II 1959-1980.* John Hohenberg is the book's editor and commentator.

Yes, in this combination chronicle and collection you'll see the results of superb reporting. But you'll see also the sort of writing that makes all journalists proud of their profession.

There's a lesson in reading the book. There's a reward.

One gains the feel *of* words and the feel *within* them. "Imagine, if you can, your skin not white but black," writes Shirley Scott in another award winner first printed by the Rochester (N.Y.) *Democrat and Chronicle:*

Imagine your present job, education, and income the same, but your family shades of brown.

The same things bother you. You worry over the possibility of war, you complain about taxes, you pay the rent and grocery bill, and you work for the health and welfare of your family.

Then how are you different from other men? Are you different?

You will soon discover that the most annoying fact of color is the ambiguity of the role you play in life. You don't feel different, yet you are treated differently. You can't justify the treatment accorded you, but you must live and cope with white justification.

And so on into the mental and emotional realm of a human being. Writing to be read. And what an ending Shirley Scott puts to her story: "The Negro walks on eggshells. The miracle of it all is his endurance."

When one mentions feeling, there comes to mind a classic, A.M. Rosenthal's 1958 award winner for the *New York Times,* "There Is No News from Auschwitz," a quiet yet gripping account of a visit to a place that never should have been but now will always be. "The most terrible thing of all, somehow," writes Rosenthal, "was that at Brzezinka the sun was bright and warm, the rows of graceful poplars were lovely to look upon, and on the grass near the gates children played."

It all seemed frighteningly wrong, as in a nightmare, that at Brzezinka the sun should ever shine or that there should be light and greenness and the sound of young laughter. It would be fitting if at Brzezinka the sun never shone and the grass withered, because this is a place of unutterable terror.

From that beginning all the way—and it is a brief if excruciating journey—to the end, when Rosenthal notes:

Into the suffocation dungeons the visitor is taken for a moment and feels himself strangling. Another visitor goes in, stumbles out, and crosses herself. There is no place to pray at Auschwitz.

The visitors look pleadingly at each other and say to the guide, "Enough."

There is nothing new to report about Auschwitz. It was a sunny day and the trees were green and at the gates the children played.

Acel Moore and Wendell Rawls, Jr. of the Philadelphia *Inquirer* make excellent use of parallelism, of repetition for emphasis, in their explosive revelation of abuses at a state mental hospital. It is a place, they say,

where men who have died in this way (beatings) have been certified as victims of heart attacks.

It is a place where men have been pummeled bloody and senseless—for sport.

It is a place where an unwritten code requires all the guards present to hit a patient if one guard hits him.

It is a place where patients have been forced to commit sodomy with guards and other patients.

It is a place where men have been forced to live naked for years on end, sometimes handcuffed on icy floors.

And so on through a litany of awfulness. The impact is considerable. As is the description in the story about a strip mine from the Louisville *Courier-Journal:* "The first visit to a strip mine is a chilling voyage into a grotesque twilight zone that combines Dante's Inferno, the wastelands of the Far West, and a horror movie. Man shrinks into insignificance alongside giant mining machines, mammoth coal trucks, towering high-walls of broken, jagged rock, and sprawling spoilbanks of lifeless soil."

Sometimes it's a phrase or a sentence that strikes the mind, as when the *Inquirer's* Richard Ben Cramer reports from Occupied Lebanon. "Here, everything is frozen in time, like a Pompeii without the lava."

Sometimes it's a section, and let me quote from one. Mary McElroy's "Rhetoric and Watergate," done for the Washington *Star* in 1974:

Enough has been said about the White House transcripts as the Thermopylae of language. That was a war in which words were almost wiped out. Through systematic abuse, they lost their meaning. "Protection reaction raid," one of the baser coinages, meant creating an alibi to bomb the enemy. When our former first citizen said, "I am not a crook," what he meant was, "You can't prove it." When he said, "One year of Watergate is enough," he meant the fire was getting hot.

When he said he was "trying to get to the bottom of it," he meant he was trying to get out of it.

It may be a while before the country stops reading "down" for "up" and "white" for "black."

The whole piece is worth reading. As is Russell Baker's "Why Being Serious Is Hard," in which he teaches us the difference between the words, "serious" and "solemn." "Jogging is solemn," he says, "Poker is serious." And in politics, "The rare candidate who is serious, like Adlai Stevenson, is easily overwhelmed by one who is solemn, like General Eisenhower." Baker hammers his point with a list of such distinctions. It includes:

Shakespeare is serious. David Susskind is solemn.
Chicago is serious. California is solemn.
Falling in love, getting married, having children, getting divorced, and fighting over who gets the car and the Wedgewood is serious. The new sexual freedom is solemn.

Playboy is solemn. The *New Yorker* is serious.

There's narration in this collection, and description, and comment. There's just awfully good reading from which I'm learning about writing all over again.

It all depends upon point of view

"I'm demanding," says the boss. "He's impossible," says his employee.

A *statesman* one calls that person in public life who's admired. A *politician* one calls that person who's not.

Is the person a *disciple* or an *apple polisher?* Is she *charming* or *without depth? Conservative* or *reactionary? Liberal* or *radical? A person of standards* or *hypercritical? Helpful* or *hurtful?*

It all depends upon the point of view.

And that point of view can be expressed both in the words you select and in the approach you take while covering a story.

In *say* versus *shout,* and *cry* versus *shriek.* Be careful to say what you want to say in the way you want to say it. Even then you cannot be sure that your reader will receive your message just the way you sent it, but at least you can improve your chances.

Think not only about *what* you're writing but *how* you're writing it. And in so doing, consider your purpose for writing. Consider your audience, too. What is it you want to tell your audience, and *how* do you offer the *what* so that the intended audience accepts the message, pays attention, acts?

Clarence Darrow considered. He was called upon to address prisoners at the Cook County Jail in Illinois. He could have talked about crime and punishment. He could have talked about repentance. He could have talked about law and justice. But would his listeners have listened? Instead, he said:

> If I looked at jails and crimes and prisoners in the way the ordinary person does, I should not speak on this subject to you. The reason I talk to you on the question of crime, its cause and cure, is because I really do not in the least believe in crime. There is no such thing as a crime as the word is generally understood. I do not believe there is any sort of distinction between the real moral condition of the people in and out of jail. One is just as good as the other. The people here can no more help being here than the people outside can avoid being outside. I do not believe that people are in jail because they deserve to be. They are in jail simply because they cannot avoid it on account of circumstances which are entirely beyond their control and for which they are in no way responsible.

I'm sure Darrow had his listeners. He understood.

As must you. Know your audience. Then select words and approach to suit the occasion.

I was reminded of the problem and the challenge recently when a good friend returned from Northern Ireland, where he had videotaped material for a cable television program. Having kept abreast of events there through our newspapers, he was prepared for the worst. And what did he see? "Well," he says, "certainly not what I expected. There are pockets of trouble, isolated spots. But most of Northern Ireland is calm and seemingly contented. The press, our press, magnifies. And, of course, those who most desire change seek out the press. They seem to perform for the cameras. That's not to say there isn't some awful bitterness, but it's far from the all-encompassing situation we're led to think exists."

It's all from the point of view. And it's much from what we want our readers to experience through our words.

Who's right, to take another "for instance," in coverage of the recent outbursts of passion in England? *Newsweek* or *The Economist?*

Newsweek notes:

> As the temper and fires of rioting finally began to smolder out last week, Britain began to come to grips with its own shattered vision of itself. Unarmed bobbies, gentle symbols of a nonviolent society, had become aggressive riot cops, flooding into troubled areas behind visored crash helmets. Their commanders took instant courses in riot control from British experts in Northern Ireland, and were granted permission to use tear gas, water cannons and plastic bullets—all virtually unheard of in England. Courts dealt with rioters quickly and harshly amid demands that trial by jury be temporarily suspended. An army camp was converted to a prison to handle the overflow from the biggest group of inmates in British history.

The Economist put it this way:

> It has not been a good two weeks for the Englishman's reputation for understatement. Many foreigners reading the headlines and watching television might have thought large areas of Britain's major cities were engulfed in street violence and anarchy.

"Police Face Bomb Blitz"; "Mob Rule Grips Cities"; "How Much More Must We Take?"; "A Rioter's Date With Terror"; "To Think This Is England!" In reality, a few small areas of a few cities suffered for a few hours; each city rarely more than once. Media distortion may have given Americans, South Africans, and even Ulstermen a wry smile, seeing the tables at last turned on British complacency about urban violence.

The media may or may not. The point is that words can be chosen to make a chosen impression upon a readership.

Just as *Time* chose to have its readers view the royal wedding as a fairy tale romance involving "a dashing Prince Charming" and "the winsome daughter of an earl," while *New York* magazine writer Marie Brenner approached the event through a garden party with participants "frozen there in a kind of eternal tableau." Frozen, ah yes. Not much romance suggested.

In Nashville *The Tennessean* editorialized: "In another section of this newspaper today appears an advertisement by the American Atheists offering a sample issue of their magazine and a number of informational packets. . . .This newspaper does not subscribe to the thoughts expressed in the ad. . . ."

To which a staffer, Dolph Honicker, responded:

> Elsewhere in the paper were ads for swingers, ads for like-new used cars, ads for palm readers, ads for chiropractors, ads for miracle diet pills and ads for miracle evangelists.
>
> Did we apologize for running those ads? No. So why did we apologize for running the almost invisible atheist ad? . . .
>
> I can only speculate.
>
> And while speculating, meditating, dozing, and pondering, I pontificate thusly:
>
> ● Atheists did not man the racks at the Inquisition.
>
> ● Atheists did not burn witches at Salem.
>
> ● It is not atheist terrorists who are starving themselves to death in Ireland.
>
> ● It is not atheists who are killing British soldiers

and blowing up innocent men and women.

And so on. It's all from the point of view, from the approach, from the material writers select, from the words they use.

We must be careful to achieve what we want.

And we must be careful also to want for our readers what's right for them. As communicators we can distort and confuse, magnify when we should diminish or diminish when we should magnify. If we're not careful, we're likely to be led to verbal excess or emotional zeal by something in the news that gives us a wallop.

When the Pope was attacked in Rome, the press responded massively and far from passively. Understandably but not always appropriately. We were reminded repeatedly that ours is an age of violence and moral sickness. The perspective of history was ignored in the rush of coverage. But then an editorial writer for the *New York Times* stopped to think. He wrote, in part:

> Society is infused with the vain idea that now is best, or worst, or most important. . . .
>
> It is a vanity that denies us the slim comfort of history. The pendulum of violence swings to mysterious rhythms, but swing it does. Consider the plots and deaths of the 1580's in Europe. . . the bombs and goons and Molly Maguires of America a century ago. . .the explosive years before World War I.
>
> Did lunacy reach some new plateau with the attack on Ronald Reagan so soon after he took office? In 1933, a 5-foot-1-inch bricklayer named Joseph Zangara shot at President-elect Roosevelt but hit Chicago Mayor Anton Cermak instead. "I do not hate Mr. Roosevelt personally," he said. "I hate all presidents, no matter from what country they come, and I hate all officials and everybody who is rich.". . .

Perspective. Through care or design or both a writer provides it (or fails to). There is power in what we do.

Consider your words

On the front of a big-city newspaper I spotted a story about a decrease in the nation's balance-of-payments deficit. Economists say the state of such a deficit has a considerable impact on our financial health. It's important, in another word. The newspaper editor apparently agreed; he put the story on page one.

Here's a typical slice of information from the story:

> The department said the main reason for the improvement was a $3.4 billion decline in the size of the U.S. merchandise trade deficit and a $300 million rise in net service receipts. . . .

> Claims on foreigners reported by U.S. banks decreased $1.4 billion, compared with a $6.3 billion first-quarter increase.

> "The decrease largely reflected a rise in U.S. short-term interest rates relative to short-term rates abroad, the strength of domestic loan demand and heightened competition in international lending," the department said.

> Net capital outflow for U.S. direct investments abroad was $4.2 billion. . . .

Wonderful stuff. "Merchandise trade deficit." "Net service receipts." "Claims on foreigners." "Domestic loan demand." "Net capital outflow." The concept of balance of payments, not within every reader's grasp, remains undefined, and on top of that we get all those fiscal phrases.

I didn't come across the story in the *Wall Street Journal,* remember, or *Business Week* where quite likely the reading audience can cope with such sludge. But in a metropolitan daily?

The editor in charge should have been dismissed for negligence. So, too, the wire service editor who permitted the story to hit the wire in that fashion (it was credited to a wire service to the discredit of that wire service). So, too, the reporter or writer who took the material from a Commerce Department release and failed to ask the government operative to translate it into English. So, too, the Commerce press representative who prepared the dang thing.

On page one of his astute and delightful book, *Strictly Speaking,* Edwin Newman asks: "Will America be the death of English? I'm glad I asked me that. My well-thought-out mature judgment is that it will. The outlook is dire."

Indeed, it is, considering the preparation and marketing of such as the above story. Newman, to press his point, later quotes a business memo: "The major thrust of Youth Services Agency's recommendations to maximize the quality and efficiency of services rendered revolve around the necessity for more phone channels. Two additional phone channels would compensate greatly for both communicative and space difficulties and such implementation is strongly urged as an immediate necessity."

How many like that have you read? Worse yet, how many like it have you written? None, I hope. But there better be no more from you in the future, comprende?

Jargon and junque, I call it, caused in part by too many of us not knowing better, caused also by the rest of us trying to show off our verbal profundity. It's a desire to achieve status, this structuring of convoluted sentences with confusing words.

And thus we have to replicate rather than duplicate or repeat. We have to explicate rather than explain. We have to facilitate rather than make things easier. We have to conflagrate rather than set on fire.

A United Technology advertisement in the *Wall Street Journal* told us to "Keep It Simple" and developed its lesson this way:

> Strike three.
> Get your hand off my knee.
> You're overdrawn.
> Your horse won.
> Yes.
> No.
> You have the account.
> Walk.
> Don't walk.
> Mother's dead.
> Basic events
> require simple language.
> Idiosyncratically euphuistic
> eccentricities are the
> promulgators of
> triturable obfuscation.
> What did you do last night?
> Enter into a meaningful
> romantic involvement

or
fall in love?
What did you have for
breakfast this morning?
The upper part of a hog's
hind leg with two oval
bodies encased in a shell
laid by a female bird
or
ham and eggs?
David Belasco, the great
American theatrical producer,
once said, "If you can't
write your idea on the
back of my calling
card,
you don't have a clear idea."

Considering that, according to U.S. Office of Education statistics, about 25 million among our adult population are "functionally illiterate," that seems eminently good advice.

So, why do we quantify and maximize and optimize and colloquize and finalize and cognize? Why do we set parameters and establish peer groups and make longitudinal studies and build infrastructures? Why must there be throughputs and matrices, interface and symbiosis?

Tell me about attitudinalization and resource utilization, about being proactive and monolithic. And by all means put me in touch with post-Industrial America.

Here's a book I never bothered to read: *Culture as Polyphony, An Essay on the Nature of Paradigms.* Despite the forbidding title, it might have been a winner. But who'd bother looking for it after the promotional copy: "This book is a fascinating diagnosis of twentieth-century consciousness. It ranges sure-footedly

from philosophical and scientific speculation through developments in popular culture, connecting present to past, past to present. . . . Culture, cultural change, and the role of art in society are the author's most general concerns. . . .In defining the non-linear paradigm that characterizes postmodern cognition, he distinguishes between Newtonian and Einsteinian physics. He traces the intellectual genesis of the nonlinear to German romantic philosophy. . . .''

Forget it.

In fact, forget academese and businessese and legalese and burocratese and scientese.

Think plain.

That's not writing down to your audience. That's writing to it and for it.

Perhaps you remember George Orwell's classic perversion of a gem, the one which read:

Objective consideration of contemporary phenomena compels the conclusion that success or failure in competitive activities exhibits no tendency to be commensurate with innate capacity, but that a considerable element of the unpredictable must invariably be taken into account.

A challenge? Yes, but of the wrong sort. The challenge should be in the thought itself (as Orwell, of course, is suggesting), and in the language as it was actually written:

I returned and saw under the sun, that the race is not to the swift, nor the battle to the strong, neither yet bread to the wise, nor yet riches to men of understanding, nor yet favor to men of skill; but time and chance happeneth to them all.

Write. Don't garble.

Boring needn't be

The saying, "There are no boring stories, only boring writers," amounts to hyperbole, of course. All of us know there are some terribly boring items out there waiting to be done. This appointment and that retirement. This survey result and that earnings report. This hum-drum speech and that dreary meeting.

But.

But the good writer, the industrious writer, the unsatisfied writer will seek out the slightly different approach, will hunt for the unusual turn of phrase, will strive for language that commands reader attention.

The better business publications provide object lessons. So do other better publications when they deal with mundane matters.

They prove that dreary stories need not be.

The *New York Times* "Business People" section proves almost every day, for instance, that the appointment or promotion story can be written with style and at least a touch of the unpredictable.

Here are some typical—yet for the genre *un*typical—leads:

An engineer will replace a lawyer in the front office of ICI Americans, the Wilmington, Del., subsidiary of Britain's Imperial Chemical Industries.

The philosopher-king is giving way to the lord-in-waiting at the Xerox Corporation: C. Peter McColough, the company's chief executive since 1968, said yesterday that he would step aside next May and that his longstanding heir apparent, David T. Kearns, would take command.

Warren Hirsh has a new job. Again. The apparel company executive, who in the past two years has seemed to change jobs as frequently as his industry changes fashions, has been named president of J. Breed Clothing Inc., a manufacturer of jeans under the Jesse Jeans label.

Ever since W. Clement Stone's son resigned last March as chief executive officer of the company his father founded, the Combined International Corporation, analysts have been wondering about how a successor might be found who shared the positive mental attitude Mr. Stone had promulgated. That question has apparently been resolved through the planned acquisition by Combined

of the Ryan Insurance Group Inc., another direct sales insurance concern.

Advertising Age does more of the same:

When the nominating committee of the Advertising Club of New York informed Judy Guerin de Neco that she was up for re-election as a vp, she turned a deaf ear.

Having held the vp post for three years, she felt it was time to make a run at the presidency. She had informed the nominating committee of that desire and her resolve not to accept any lesser position.

Judy Guerin de Neco, president of Judy Guerin Associates, was determined to get her way. And she did.

Ms. Guerin de Neco is the first woman president of the New York Adclub, following the club's first heated election in its 67-year history.

Suddenly I'm interested. If it had been written by the numbers, I couldn't have cared less.

Decent beginnings to stories well written throughout, stories that could have been the usual bores.

"Steel industry leaders believe that their fight against imports has taken a modest step forward —and a big step backward," writes a writer for *Industry Week*. The story is all about imports of non-tubular steel. A real winner. Well, it actually is because the writer refused to let himself think that the subject was worth no more than the usual treatment. He decided the story does not have to be a bore, indeed that it should not be because the subject is important to his readers. So, he worked with his words to make them more winning.

What do you say about a clean restaurant kitchen? If you write for *Restaurant Hospitality,* then you might put it this way:

If cleanliness is indeed next to godliness, then the kitchen at Tony's belongs not in St. Louis but high atop Olympus, wherefrom its pleasures could be whisked to the table of Zeus. This is the sort of kitchen that gives Inspectors of Health bad dreams about pink slips and unemployment lines, for if every kitchen were maintained so meticulously, we would have no need of them or their rules. The Health Code could go on the Honor System.

At the very least, less boring writers write less boring stories. They're not satisfied to do things the way things usually are done.

Forbes, in Malcolm S.'s column, "Fact and Comment," gives oomph to what could be oomphless material. Mr. Forbes likes to let a headline be part of a lead. "If anybody should have nuclear plant neurosis," is his boldfaced introduction to a story that continues the statement in regular body type. "If anybody should have nuclear plant neurosis it's the Japanese, as the atomization of Hiroshima and Nagasaki gave them a firsthand, horrific experience of what that warhead could do even in its earliest, crudest, least powerful form as a weapon. Yet in Japan today there are 16 atomic energy plants in operation and they have announced plans to build 19 more." It's a not-the-usual way of introducing the acceptance of nuclear power overseas.

The thoughtful writer looks for the unusual element, or for context, or for the twist of words that lifts the story out of the commonplace. Geoffrey Colvin faced the problem in one of *Fortune's* many financial profiles of companies. Growth figures are growth figures, after all. With all their differences, they tend to sound the same. But he wrote:

> In business, as in nature, there seems to be a law that things slow down as they grow toward the elephantine. Now 25 years old and with annual revenues of $3.2 billion, Digital Equipment Corp., the Maynard, Massachusetts, maker of minicomputers, continues blithely to ignore that law, to the increasing astonishment of investors and competitors. DEC's revenues have grown at an average annual rate of 36 percent over the last decade. Restrained by the recession, they'll probably rise a mere 25 percent this fiscal year, which ends July 3. What's more, DEC has achieved this staggering expansion without ever acquiring another company.

A contextual wrapping gives DEC's success story more meaning. It also makes the reading more engrossing.

Think for attractiveness. Think for meaning. Think for the unusual.

And that means don't review a book called *Interdisciplinarity and Higher Education* by saying: "The ten contributors to this volume are currently or formerly associates of interdisciplinary programs at Pennsylvania State University, where a senior in 1975-76 initiated these essays. They are from several disciplines and their approaches vary widely. As the preface notes, the results 'neither exhaust the subject or constitute a harmonious whole.' They do convey the scope of the topic, considerable information, and some differing points of view."

That sort of writing needs to go on a diet. How heavy can you get?

Better something like:

Multidisciplinary.

Pluridisciplinary.

Interdisciplinary.

Crossdisciplinary.

Transdisciplinary.

All from the language of higher education. If you want to find out what they mean and how they relate, then *Interdisciplinarity and Higher Education* should give you a good start.

It's not the final word, as editor Joseph Kockelmans advises in his preface. The materials "neither exhaust the subject nor constitute a harmonious whole." But the collection offers scope. It's informative. And a range of opinions gets expressed.

I might still seek to skip the book. But such a review gives the work a chance.

Which leads me to Citibank, "New York's biggest." I give Citibank credit for an effort to make a boring subject lively. I quote:

> One of the most prominent figures in twentieth century banking never accepted a deposit. He earned his reputation by making withdrawals. Willie Sutton (1901-1980) staged his first bank robbery in 1927 and in the following years held up more than twenty additional banks. He was arrested five times and served a total of 35 years in various prisons before retiring in 1969. When asked at the height of his career why he robbed banks, Sutton is reported to have looked incredulous and replied, "That's where the money is."

> Were Willie Sutton to take up his career today, he wouldn't find it all that simple. Today, he'd have

to case a dazzling variety of institutions to ply his trade.

And we then find out about that dazzling variety.

Here's another example from the same Citibank presentation:

Eighty years ago, payments were made through long distance shipments of money. Butch and Sundance discovered a weakness in the delivery system and made tens of thousands of dollars intercepting money in transit, by robbing trains.

That was a fairly simple task. Trains always followed the same tracks, and tried diligently to approximate their announced schedules as well.

Today money travels at the speed of light, through air and through telephone lines. You can't intercept it in transit.

We then find out about today's money in transit.

All this, and more, can be found in Citibank's "Old Bank Robbers' Guide to Where the New Money Is." Jesse James and Pretty Boy Floyd and Ma Barker and John Dillinger and all the rest of them get their just attention in the pages of this entertaining *and* informative booklet about safety and security in the banking system today. A basically not-too-interesting subject for most of us. But Citibank's approach makes one pay heed. It can be interesting, after all. A writer has proved it.

As you can, no matter how seemingly sleep-inducing the subject, if you try. It's not enough just to get yourself through a story. You have to get your readers through it. To do that, remember: boring needn't be.

A story needs structure

First the writer must provide a lead which gains attention and suggests content.

"Other work is death to writing; a writer needs to be obsessive."

So says a novelist.

And yet about half of those who consider themselves authors work only part-time at their craft.

"I'd give up my job by day's end if my writing would support me."

So says a writer of non-fiction.

And yet she cannot because her annual take from writing is $5,000, "and who can live on that?"

Once a writer gets underway, he or she should turn to thesis—a sentence or paragraph that tells precisely and pithily what the story will cover.

Not a lot of writers, which is why, according to "The Columbia University Survey of American Authors," the profession of writing in this country has become largely part-time.

Response from 2,239 authors producing books of fiction and non indicate that the author's lot is not a happy one.

Elaboration follows: meat, substance, support material for the article's thesis. Here the writer takes from his bag of tricks all the narrative and descriptive powers at his command, the structural devices, the expositional techniques to keep the reader interested and to get that reader informed. Just how the writer elaborates depends on subject matter and situation, but the result sought is reader involvement.

The average annual intake is approximately $4,775 or "about two-thirds of the maximum amount paid to individuals on Social Security," according to Robert Merton, one of the study's collaborators.

By the hour, the average writer earns $4.90. But half of those who responded to the survey have hourly incomes less than that. "On the average, writing yields little economic return," conclude the Columbia University social scientists who amassed enough information to pack 150 pages with statistics and analysis, thus providing the most detailed picture ever made of how those who've had at least one book published make out or make do.

Among the details:

- 31 per cent of our full-time authors, those who spend more than 25 hours per week writing and hold no other jobs, earn less than $5,000. Two-thirds make less than $20,000.
- That average earnings figure of $4,775 would be considerably lower were it not for top authors who make five and six figure sums.
- Genre fiction writers do better than the others. These creators of Gothics and romances, detective stories and westerns include among them 20 per cent with incomes over $50,000. And yet 40 per cent earn less than $5,000.
- An author's income varies greatly from year to year. For instance, in 1979 (the year covered by the study) five per cent earned 10 times from their writing what they had the previous year, while another five per cent earned one fifth of their 1978 income.

Respondents expressed concerns about making ends meet, about publishers, publicists, and public.

"It's a depressing situation," says one writer. "We have to work to write when we'd rather write as work."

"The place is a supermarket," says another about the size and impersonality of a publishing house.

"I went to twelve cities on my book tour and never saw a copy," comments a third about unfocused promotional work done in her behalf.

"What can you expect? They're all watching cop shows," pronounces a fourth gloomily about the decline and disappearance of the reading public.

As a story needs a beginning, so it needs an ending; the little twist of insight, the touch of satire, the evocation of a mood to be remembered, or perhaps just an informational tidbit that summarizes what came before. Again, the method and selection depend on the purpose of the story as well as on what the readers are likely to accept. But an end should be that. Conclusive. Clear cut.

As much as all this matters, it doesn't seem to matter. Ninety-four per cent of the responding authors say they intend to keep on writing. And so it will always be because writers need to write.

And so with articles it usually is: an introduction or lead, a theme or thesis, an elaboration or body, a summary or conclusion. Structure helps a reader end.

The end.

The tandem

Like ham and eggs, like shoes and socks, like catcher and pitcher, writing and reporting fit together. They're a tandem.

It takes careful and thorough reporting to make a good story. And the professional writer will make sure that the story flows naturally out of the gathered material.

Ira Berkow did in his story for the *New York Times,* one that required sensitivity because of subject matter and because it concerned a troubled young man, one capable of being a hero but uncomfortably wearing the image of a villain, at least for a period of time.

Berkow's is a cleanly written article, lean, without the clutter of unnecessary words or tricks. He's obviously thought about the information he gathered, then permitted it to flow. The result is a story shaped by and from the material.

The particulars of the Berkow piece will date. The dilemma posed will not. Neither will the method he's used to form a most readable and engrossing article: to let the facts determine structure.

The Bulls recently conducted a three-day camp in Chicago for their rookies, but their top draft choice, Quintin Dailey, was not there. Team officials had determined that it was best that he not show up. The climate in Chicago, explained the Bulls' managing partner, Jonathan Kovler, was "too inflammatory."

The lead is based on a news peg, the signing of a ballplayer, the opening of training camp, and the incongruity of the "star" being absent. Those are the main facts. Together they're intriguing enough to make a plain training camp story a feature. Notice also the strong touch of quote: "too inflammatory." That's just enough to make us go on. An excellent lead, sufficiently factual and organized to arouse our interest.

In the last seven months, Quintin Dailey has traveled a most dizzying and ugly odyssey. He now seeks, he says, "a new beginning." He hopes for the climate in Chicago to cool by the season opener in October.

Dailey, a 6-foot-3-inch all-America guard from the University of San Francisco, pleaded guilty in June to reduced charges of aggravated assault and

false imprisonment of a nursing student who lived in the same dormitory as he did at the university. Three additional charges, all sex-related, had been dropped as a result of plea bargaining.

Dailey was considered the best guard available in the National Basketball Association draft, a 21-year-old junior who had decided to forego his last year of college eligibility. But, because of the crime to which he had admitted, it was uncertain which team, if any, would draft him.

The Bulls chose him in the first round. But when he went to a news conference to introduce himself to the Chicago press, he seemed unrepentant—even flippant—and was assailed in the papers as a person who ought to be "hated."

The Bulls' front office was rocked. Angry fans called to say they would never go to another game. Women's groups picketed, and one irate woman said on radio that if Dailey came to Chicago no woman would be safe on the streets.

The player's absence is explained. The "too inflammatory" is explained. Here is the background, that which led to the ironic non-event. In compression Berkow gives us what we need to know, no fine points yet but the basics. The second paragraph of the story, the first of the section quoted above, is beautifully crafted. It serves as thesis, telling us briefly what the whole story is about. And the phrase, "a most dizzying and ugly odyssey," is so appropriate to the facts and to the spirit of the story. The remaining paragraphs follow smoothly, one after the other, taking us to the furor of phone calls and public concern. We come to understand why Quintin Dailey was missing, why his new bosses decided to keep him out of the limelight.

Sometime later, after he had seen the reaction to the news conference, Dailey pleaded for understanding. He said that he had been confused, that he had wished to look to the future rather than linger on the past. That's what he had tried, unsuccessfully, to communicate. And yes, he was sorry about what had happened. He said he was happy only that he was being given an opportunity to play basketball again.

Dailey has said that all he asks is a chance to show that he is "a human being and not an animal."

Here we have the young man's reaction to the

reaction, his explanation, his "what I meant to say," his plea to be understood. Berkow wants to make sure that various and varying sides are heard. Dailey's words alter the tone of the story. The reader is likely to shift emotional gear just a bit. Why, maybe he's just a misguided, mixed-up, and inarticulate kid. It leads us to want to know more about him, to find out how he got to where he is, a gifted athlete and a criminal.

> Indeed, before this, Dailey had a reputation as a young man to be respected, even admired. "He was," said a reporter in San Francisco, "someone who seemed to be making something of his life despite hardships."
> Dailey grew up in a Baltimore ghetto, and, between his sophomore and junior years in high school, both of his parents died of illnesses. He was reared by an aunt in Baltimore.
> He discovered that he possessed a marvelous gift for bouncing a round ball and tossing it through a hoop. A lot of people got excited about this, and, as is the case with many outstanding athletes in our country, he was raised to celebrity status.
> He was courted by innumerable institutions of higher learning—not as a potential Nobel laureate, but because he might help the basketball team make money. He decided on San Francisco, 3,000 miles from his home.

More of our questions about Dailey are answered. The good youngster. The ghetto youngster. The by-the-bootstrap youngster. And the schools that wanted him. Here is the context of his life: poverty, the search for a way out, and those who would help him while also using him. The crime element may not be typical, but otherwise this seems to be a classic tale oft told in 20th century America, the making of a sports hero. And we get a hint of the pressure that burdens such young people when they seek their way out, a pressure which in this case may have been too much. Berkow doesn't even hint at mercy for the fellow. He's merely letting the story unfold, letting the facts speak for themselves, letting readers come to their own conclusions.

> At the school, he was treated like few scholars. In fact, one alumnus gave him a summer job paying $1,000 a month, and he never had to go to it.
> When university officials learned of the payoffs,

they began an internal investigation into the school's basketball program, which had been on probation by the National Collegiate Athletic Association twice in the last three years. The investigation resulted in the discovery of other improprieties and, last week, the dropping of the sport.

Here we get the school story. It is further explanation of what Dailey experienced before the fateful event. By now there's a suspense to the article. We know where we're going, and yet we don't. We know what will happen because we've already been told what happened, and yet we sort of hope that maybe it won't happen, that maybe the story will turn out differently in the paragraphs ahead. It doesn't, of course. It cannot, and in that is the tragedy.

> Dailey's troubles began around 3:45 A.M. on Monday, Dec. 21, 1981. The files in court say that Dailey forced his way into the room of a nursing student, a residence adviser in the dormitory, someone he had known only casually and who had not been flirtatious with him. Dailey was there several hours, and the night of terror for the young woman ended only when he fell asleep and she ran out to get help. When she returned, he was gone.
> At first, Dailey said he didn't do it. Then he agreed to a plea bargain. "The draft was coming up," said his agent, Bob Woolf of Boston, "and we thought that if the case were hanging over his head, this chance for him to play in the N.B.A. might be lost forever."
> Dailey was given three years of probation, rather than a jail sentence, because the judge, Edward Stern, considered Dailey's record of no previous offenses, the severity of the crime as he understood it and a letter from the victim to the judge.

The crime is committed. We find out more about it and learn of the aftermath. The handling of the information is straightforward, carefully written by Berkow, without much in the way of featurized treatment. These are the facts, he's telling us. Here's why the Bulls have a problem on their hands. Here is Quintin Dailey's problem, his record, a part of his life that cannot be removed no matter what feats he accomplishes in his future. But what now? The story is not complete. As a reader, I wonder about the woman, the victim. And I wonder about what next. Here's how Berkow ends:

> "I am in complete agreement with the plea bargaining which has taken place," she wrote. "I feel that probation will serve as a constant reminder to Quintin of his mistake, and I highly doubt that he will make the same mistake again. . . .I feel justice was served as long as his probation is supervised."

Should Dailey be given a chance now to return to basketball, to earn a lot of money, to "begin again?"

There are two arguments:

How would you feel, goes the first, if she were your daughter?

The other is, how would you feel if he were your son?

That answers questions while still leaving them. The windup is powerful. Let's not jump to opinions. The events, the people involved, are worthy of more thought.

Berkow gives no value judgments. He's carried us expertly through the facts. What he learned we now know. What he thinks we do not. Instead, he's urging us to. Reporting and writing in tandem. And now it's all supposed to churn in our minds. That's good journalism.

How much to cover

When you picked up this book, you certainly didn't expect to read about Franz Joseph Haydn.

But then, why not? A publication about writing should be open to anything.

Besides, I'm going to use "Papa" Haydn to make a point, a suitable one in my view for you, our readers.

You'll read a lot about Haydn in 1982, if you look for him, just as you'll read a lot about Igor Stravinsky, just as you'll read less but still more than usual about some other composers of note.

Reason?

Anniversaries. You know, the round kind. It'll be the 250th of Haydn's birth, the 100th of Stravinsky's.

Now, for an article subject I thought about such anniversaries, composer anniversaries. A bit of research disclosed that 1982 marks the 450th anniversary of Orlando di Lasso's birth, and the 350th of Jean Baptiste Lully, and the 200th of Nicolo Paganini and Daniel Auber, and the 100th of Zoltan Kodaly and Karol Szymanowski, all in addition to Haydn and Stravinsky.

Potentially interesting subject, the year's anniversaries. But on reconsideration, what really could I cover if I covered that little universe? Could I give adequate space to tidbits of life and love on each of these fellows, some of whom—believe me—had fascinating stays on earth?

There's my point.

Could I in such a wrapup tell you Haydn was the most revered composer of his age, as well as teacher and friend of Mozart and teacher of Beethoven?

Could I tell you he's called Father of the Symphony and that really he should also be called Father of the Sonata and Father of the String Quartet because he developed and refined these as well?

Could I tell you he didn't always take himself too seriously and that he explained the discrepancy of his birthdate (he said it was March 31; the town registry said April 1) by suggesting, "I preferred to claim. . .March 31 because I didn't want people to say I came into the world as an April fool?"

Could I tell you of his unhappy and often hungry childhood, of his 30 years as house composer for a noble Hungarian family (his contract called for him to "behave soberly" and "have all his musicians at all times clean" and "to compose such music as His Serene Highness may require of him")?

Could I tell you he wrote 1,047 compositions including an astounding 104 symphonies, 83 string quartets, and 23 operas? Could I tell you how he composed and how he liked to fish?

Could I tell you the story about his "Farewell" Symphony, how he wrote it as a lesson to his prince who refused to permit musicians' families to visit the estate while he was in residence and then wouldn't leave, causing stress and causing their beloved leader, Haydn, to react with a symphony in which during the final movement the musicians symbolically leave the stage one by one until none is left?

Could I tell you about Haydn and London, Haydn and patriotism, Haydn and a space opera, Haydn and the avant-garde, Haydn and his "Surprise" Symphony?

No. Not and also do the same for that seminal 20th Century composer Stravinsky, and so forth.

It would be too much of a good thing and—consequently—not enough. In an effort to cover everything I would fail to cover anything.

Decisions must be made, decisions based on how much territory can be adequately covered so that the major questions readers might ask are answered.

I say don't try to cover too much. In my situation, better to stick to Haydn and really let my readers meet him. Then, perhaps, I could do a series of articles, one on each composer on my anniversary list.

You can decide that the new benefits package is worth a series of articles, one on life insurance, another on hospitalization, a third on major medical, a fourth on special benefits, a fifth on retirement.

You can decide that the senior management team deserves a series of profiles rather than lumping into one; that the new corporate headquarters should be treated in an entire issue of articles rather than in a single piece; that the university's research efforts should be packaged across several months of alumni magazines.

That way, as I said, questions can be answered. And the flavor of the subject can be captured.

And the details which readers relate to and remember can be included.

That way also you can help solve a problem common to a lot of editors, the one of filling space.

Remember "Papa" Haydn. Give *your* "Papa" Haydn the space he deserves.

'Never send an adjective on a noun's errand'

"The waters deluge man with rain, oppress him with hail, and drown him with inundations," wrote Pliny the Elder some 2,000 years ago.

He didn't burden his verbalizations with adjectives. He understood the values of nouns and verbs. And that understanding makes his paean to our earth so pungent:

> . . .the air rushes in storms, prepares the tempest, or lights up the volcano; but the earth, gentle and indulgent, ever subservient to the wants of man, spreads his walks with flowers, and his table with plenty; returns, with interest, every good committed to her care; and though she produces poison, she still supplies the antidote; though constantly teased more to furnish the luxuries of man than his necessities, yet even to the last she continues her kind indulgence, and, when life is over, she piously covers his remains in her bosom.

Writers need to remember that lesson, as did his son, Pliny the Younger, when he provided the only written account of that momentous event in 79 A.D., of an earth in eruptive fury burying a city, Pompeii:

> We saw the sea sucked away by the heaving of the earth. . .a fearful black cloud forked with great tongues of fire lashed at the heavens and torrents of ash began to pour from the sky.

> Although it was daytime, we were enveloped by night—not a moonless night or one dimmed by cloud—but the darkness of a sealed room without light.

These two ancient examples prove the power of specificity supplied by nouns and their verbs, preferable language tools to those modifiers we call adjectives. The adjective is so easily beckoned. Its careless user can create sentences stuffed with baggage, yet empty of meaning. The adjective poorly used generalizes and trivializes.

For instance, to say a boy is oh, so young, is to say oh, so much less than he's 20 and acts ¾ his age.

To describe a street fair as busy, colorful, extensive, multi-faceted, and international is to tell the reader virtually nothing. The writer keeps his reader distant and uninformed. So much better to have brought out the specifics, the more visible graphics which come from nouns and verbs. Then the air could hold, enfold aromas of incense and honey. The palate can savor curry and the tartness of lingonberries, baklava and sour pork, pepper-laden tacos and an orange ice cream that emphasizes the cream. For the eyes and mind exhibits stretch for two miles. Books about aerodynamics and zoology. Toe shoes and white elephant trinkets, belts, buckles, and beads, pottery from New Mexico's Indians to quilts from the ladies of Ashtabula, Ohio. The crowd can be described more precisely through individuals than as a mass. Entertainers, more precisely, become jugglers, dancers of the tango, and steel band magicians. Yes, and balloons need mention along with the T-shirts sporting "Fair-thee-well," donkey rides, and clowns on stilts.

Of course, nouns and verbs can go awry, too. They need careful selection and tending lest they become too general, too imprecise. A scalpel tells us more than knife, maroon more than red, and mongrel more than dog. Saunter and simper may say more than walk and talk, but only if those words accurately convey the action.

John Ciardi, in one of those priceless columns on writing for *Saturday Review,* once said: "Never send an adjective on a noun's errand." It's good advice.

John Steinbeck knew. In his *Travels with Charley* he relates the struggle to change a tire in mud:

> I lay on my stomach and edged my way, swam my way under the truck, holding my nostrils clear of the surface of the water. The jack handle was slippery with greasy mud. Mud balls formed in my beard. I lay panting like a wounded duck, quietly cursing as I inched the jack forward under an axle that I had to find by feel, since it was under water. Then, with superhuman gruntings and bubblings, my eyes starting from their sockets, I levered the great weight. I could feel my muscles tearing apart and separating from their anchoring bones. In actual time, not over an hour elapsed before I had the spare tire on. I was unrecognizable under many layers of yellow mud. My hands were cut and bleeding. I rolled the bad tire to a high place and inspected it. The whole side wall had blown out. Then I looked at the left rear tire, and to my horror saw a great rubber bubble on its side and farther along, another. It was obvious that the other tire might go at any moment, and it was

Sunday and it was raining and it was Oregon. If the other tire blew, there we were, on a wet and lonesome road, having no recourse except to burst into tears and wait for death. And perhaps some kind birds might cover us with leaves.

Adjectives are not needed when there are gruntings and bubblings and muscles tearing apart.

Pain is the subject of a gripping article in the *New Yorker* last April, "No Name, No Number," by Jacob Timerman (with translation from the Spanish by Tolby Talbot). The story deals with Argentine prisons, which Timerman was forced to sample. He writes:

In the long months of confinement, I often thought about how to convey the pain that a tortured person undergoes. And always I concluded that it was impossible. It is a pain without points of reference, without revelatory symbols or clues to serve as indicators. A man is shunted so quickly from one world to another that he's unable to tap a residue of energy that will permit him to confront this unbridled violence. That is the first phase of torture: to take a man by surprise, without allowing him any reflex defense, even psychological. A man's hands are shackled behind him, his eyes blindfolded. No one says a word. Blows are showered upon him. He's placed on the ground and someone counts to ten, but he's not killed. He is then led to what may be a canvas bed or a table, stripped, doused with water, and tied to the ends of the bed or table with his hands and legs outstretched. And the application of electric shocks begins. The amount of electricity transmitted by the electrodes—or whatever they're called—is regulated, so that it merely hurts, or burns, or destroys. It's impossible to shout—you howl. At the onset of that long human howl, someone with soft hands checks the state of your heart, someone sticks his hand into your mouth and pulls out your tongue in order to prevent you from choking. Someone places a piece of rubber in your mouth to prevent you from biting your tongue or destroying your lips. A brief pause. And then it starts all over again. With insults this time. A brief pause. And then questions. A brief pause. And then words of hope. A brief pause. And then insults.

What does a man feel? The only thing that comes to mind: They're ripping apart my flesh. They didn't rip apart my flesh. They didn't even leave marks. But I felt as if they were tearing my flesh. And what else? Nothing that I can think of. . . .

Barely an adjective to be seen. The words devastate.

And in the mail today came proof that even the virtuoso of the adjective, "New Journalism's" Tom Wolfe, knows that some writing problems are better solved with fewer adjectives and more and better nouns activated by verbs. The proof: his sure-to-be-controversial *From Bauhaus to Our House*, a dissection of modern architecture. As he puts it:

Every child goes to school in a building that looks like a duplicating-machine replacement-parts wholesale distribution warehouse. . . . Every new $900,000 summer house in the north woods of Michigan or on the shore of Long Island has so many pipe railings, ramps, hob-tread metal spiral stairways, sheets of industrial plate glass, banks of tungsten-halogen lamps, and white cylindrical shapes, it looks like an insecticide refinery. I once saw the owners of such a place driven to the edge of sensory deprivation by the whiteness & lightness & leanness & cleanness & bareness & spareness of it all. They became desperate for an antidote, such as coziness & color. They tried to bury the obligatory white sofas under Thai-silk throw pillows of every rebellious, iridescent shade of magenta, pink, and tropical green imaginable. . . . Every great law firm in New York moves without a sputter of protest into a glass-box office building with concrete slab floors and seven-foot-ten-inch-high concrete slab ceilings and plaster-board walls and pygmy corridors—and then hires a decorator and gives him a budget of hundreds of thousands of dollars to turn these mean cubes and grids into a horizontal fantasy of a Restoration townhouse.

Take a cue from some masters. Sharpen your nouns and verbs. Put a few more adjectives away in that bag of unused words.

The I Factor

The A-B-C's of good writing are rather well known.

A is for accuracy, and no amount of checking and double checking is too much. Someone's always out there ready to pounce should you get a fact wrong or make an improper assumption.

B is for brevity, and whatever you can do to hold length down will be appreciated by your very busy and sometimes very lazy readers.

C is for clarity, and that depends on how carefully you use the language. Gustave Flaubert may have exaggerated, but the point he makes is valid: "Whatever the thing you wish to say, there is but one word to express it, but one verb to give it movement, but one adjective to qualify it. You must seek until you find this noun, this verb, this adjective."

Reading E.B. White's *Essays* recently, and I urge you to do so if you would be engrossed and entertained by a man who knows both how to think and write, I came upon several analogies, which White uses so well and which also are a writer's device to clarify.

"I liked to sail alone," he writes in one essay. "The sea was the same as a girl to me—I did not want anyone else going."

"A poem," he tells me in his magnificent essay on New York, "compresses much in a small space and adds music, thus heightening its meaning. The city is like poetry: it compresses all life, all races and breeds, into a small island and adds music and the accompaniment of internal engines."

"A home," he concludes in still another verbal excursion, "is like a reservoir equipped with a check valve: the valve permits influx but prevents outflow." And he goes on:

Acquisition goes on night and day—smoothly, subtly, imperceptibly. I have no sharp taste for acquiring things, but it is not necessary to desire things in order to acquire them. Goods and chattels seek a man out; they find him even though his guard is up. Books and oddities arrive in the mail. Gifts arrive on anniversaries and fete days. Veterans send ballpoint pens. Banks send memo books. If you happen to be a writer, readers send whatever may be cluttering up their own lives; I had a man once send me a chip of wood that showed the marks of a beaver's teeth.

Someone dies, and a little trickle of indestructible keepsakes appears, to swell the flood. This steady influx is not counterbalanced by any comparable outgo. Under ordinary circumstances, the only stuff that leaves a home is paper trash and garbage; everything else stays on and digs in.

But enough of the A-B-C's. I set out to tell you of the I Factor.

I is for information, that which you always want to supply in abundance, lest you waste your reader's time.

I is for intelligence, that which you can dig up through your special sources so that the reader feels he's on the inside, getting the tips and tidbits that his competitors might not have (competitors in business or competitors at a cocktail party).

I is for interpretation, with which you give meaning to what otherwise might just be stray facts.

Most of all I is for interest, which is what you need to keep your readers with you: information and intelligence and interpretation *interestingly* offered.

Each story you provide should include interest factors, at least one and all the way up to 13. Let me share them, alphabetically.

(1) Competition. The sports pages are proof that competition interests people. There's no other reason for their existence. Little of lasting import happens, but people are enthralled or entertained, even temporarily uplifted, by feats accomplished by athletes. Consider the U.S. Olympic hockey team. Its accomplishments had little if any lasting impact on our lives. But what joy these young men provided over the short haul, and how we gobbled up stories about them.

(2) Conflict. The more extensive, intensive, and sometimes excessive form of competition between nations or groups of people—armies or labor and management—certainly gains our attention. Just look at a newspaper or watch television news almost any day any year any place.

(3) Controversy. Election campaigns are proof that we have an interest in differing opinions. Arguments attract, sometimes repellingly, but they do attract.

(4) Consequences. If your readers consider the event or development important, then they'll

read about it. And the more people that consider the event or development important, consequential, the more attention you'll gain for your story. Health is of consequence. Food is of consequence. Shelter is of consequence. Income is of consequence. Family and community welfare are of consequence. Beauty, comfort, leisure are of consequence. Clothing and energy are of consequence.

(5) Familiar or famous person. Get Jane Fonda to embrace your belief, as the anti-nukes have, and suddenly more people are interested, leading the press to be more interested. Get a Robert Redford to embrace your belief, as the environmentalists have, and suddenly the same thing happens. Get an Oscar Peterson to give street concerts on behalf of your bank, as a Canadian bank did not long ago, and suddenly there's a horde of reporters ready to tell a waiting public, and as a result the bank gets a lot of attention it otherwise wouldn't have.

(6) Heart strings. A child made well through treatment of a new drug, a family overcoming terrible handicaps of sightlessness or joblessness, a woman bootstrapping to get from nowhere to somewhere: the journalist knows such stories gain the reader's interest. That's why newspapers and magazines and television programs are filled with them.

(7) Humor. People like to laugh or chuckle or smile. It makes them happy. Why shouldn't writers make readers happy, when the occasion calls for it?

(8) Problem. Let there be a problem which people recognize as such, and if you write about it, they'll read. Of course, it should be a problem that your readers share, are aware of, can understand.

(9) Progress. Move ahead toward unravelling the problem, and people will want to know how and why. Progress in the fight against poverty or hunger, the fight against too much heat or cold, too much light or dark, the fight against illiteracy or incontinency: these bring you readers.

(10) Success. Of course. We're encouraged by victories, satisfied by triumphs. At the least they keep us going. At the most they keep us living.

(11) Unknown. "The heavens are telling the glory to God," goes the old hymn. We are intrigued by the heavens, why they are blue and why they are endless. We are mystified by quarks and quasars, not to speak of God. Science and technology and art and education give us the unknown. So does the sea. And deep, dark caves. And ants. And the brain.

(12) Unusual. Fidel Castro urges his Cubans to donate their bodies after death for medicine, "and in this way we'll deprive the worms of some of their food." Unusual; that interests us. Fish can laugh, we're advised. Unusual; that interests me. *People* do strange and fascinating and contradictory things. *People* make the world unusual, as well as the month and year. They fill space and time with their unusual activities and thoughts and talents, whether making musical toilet chairs to get toddlers to perform or putting tape machines at grave sites so that the departed can speak to the bereaved. We do the unusual, and the rest of us like to read about it.

(13) Want/need. Whatever we want to make our lives more pleasurable or need to make our lives more bearable or manageable, we will read about. Whatever we desire or require gets our attention. It's up to you, as writer, to show us the want and/or need.

It's up to you, as writer, to provide the I Factor, along with A, B, and C.

No one way to begin a story

A lead should lead, they say.

And so it should.

A lead should establish the subject of your article, set its tone, guide clearly into the rest of the story, and (not least significantly) attract attention.

When warring and sparring *Time* and *Newsweek* came up recently with the same cover piece, my attention was drawn quickly to the stories themselves (both well done) and to their leads. Quite different they were, narrative in the case of *Newsweek,* statistical and expository in *Time.* Effective each. Here's *Newsweek:*

They started walking at dusk, two teen-agers casually spreading the message that the streets of West Los Angeles were no longer safe. First they stopped Phillip Lerner and demanded money. Lerner had no cash, only his infant in a stroller. They let him pass and kept walking. They hailed Arkady and Rachel Muskin at a nearby intersection. The couple quickly handed over $8 and two wristwatches, and gratefully fled. Next the boys intercepted two elderly Chinese women and pulled out a pistol. When one woman tried to push the gun out of her face, ten bullets blazed out, killing both. The boys kept walking. They came upon a trio of friends out for an evening stroll. They took a watch and a few dollars and, without so much as a word, killed one of the three, a Frenchman visiting Los Angeles for the first time. The boys kept walking. At last they reached a drive-in restaurant where they found 76-year-old Leo Ocon walking on the sidewalk. They argued with him for less than a minute and then shot him down. Their evening over, they climbed into an old sedan and then, much as they had started, calmly went off into the night.

In the year that mainstream America rediscovered violent crime, that Sunday-night massacre was the paradigmatic act.

Time began:

Day by day, America's all too familiar crime clock ticks faster and faster. Every 24 minutes, a murder is committed somewhere in the U.S. Every ten seconds a house is burgled, every seven minutes a woman is raped. There is some truth in the aphorism of Charles Silberman, author of *Criminal Violence, Criminal Justice,* that "crime is as American as Jesse James." But there is also

something new about the way that Americans are killing, robbing, raping and assaulting one another. The curse of violent crime is rampant not just in the ghettos of depressed cities, where it always has been a malignant force to contend with, but everywhere in urban areas, in suburbs and peaceful countrysides. More significant, the crimes are becoming more brutal, more irrational, more random—and therefore all the more frightening.

Meaning there is no one way to begin a story. Meaning there is no best way to begin a story. Meaning there is no limitation to the creativity used save that imposed by lack of time or energy.

Let me share a few other leads I've liked of late.

Dick Teresi wrote in *Omni:*

Since Erasistratus starved a sparrow to "note the decrease in weight," billions of animals have been starved, suffocated, shocked, shot, boiled, baked, frozen, thawed, refrozen, force-fed, crucified, crashed, crushed, asphyxiated, irradiated, poisoned, and laser-beamed—all in the name of science.

Notwithstanding the countless medical breakthroughs from animal experimentation, animals are far from the ideal research tool.

The power of compression to make a point. A point has been compressed on the other hand, by Cynthia Parsons in *The Christian Science Monitor:*

They are in serious trouble, the public schools in major U.S. cities. As one school man remarked, only half in jest:

"If you think you see some light at the end of the tunnel, obviously you're going in the wrong direction."

To the *New York Times* I go for a narrative lead and a descriptive one, the first by Wendell Rawls Jr., the other by Richard Eder:

ATLANTA—Pamela Crumbey saw two men approaching as she and her little brother walked from school. She saw the men grab her brother. The 13-year-old girl fought the abductors futilely, her small fists flailing, as they took her 9-year-old brother away and left her in tears.

Then she woke up, crying.

The black teen-ager's recurring nightmare is an example of the distress and anxiety found increasingly among children in this city, where 22 black children have disappeared in the past 20 months.

And:

BUCHAREST—City winters always looked bedraggled after a while, but in Eastern Europe they are tired from the start. Bucharest has just dug and melted partway out of a 20-inch snowstorm, but the snow has not so much vanished as turned to mud, or evaporated into a persistent milky fog.

Because of the fuel shortage. . .lights have been turned off everywhere. The halls of the ministries are dark except at the stairwells, and there is just enough light in the restaurant to turn the food gray.

The other night, a two-section trolley bus, its red and yellow sides covered with grime, loomed out of the blackness. It was lit so dimly inside that the passengers were a single crowded shadow behind misted windows. The conductor hopped off to maneuver the overhead trolley onto a new line. A passerby joked:

"Suddenly you'll see a flash of light."

"Suddenly," his companion rejoined, "You'll see no conductor."

Esquire featured a "Looking at Forty" article by Digby Diehl, and he put feelings on paper clearly, feelings based on actualities:

Some guys give up their dental practice and go to Tahiti. Some have a torrid affair with a pizza waitress in a sleazy hotel. Others return to graduate school and find solace in the groves of academe. A few discover drugs and make fools of themselves freaking out. A friend of mine had a complete mental breakdown, a trip to the funny farm, and a revitalized reentry into respectable upper-middle-class life, and his corporation never got wind of it. One way or another, we must all face a middle-age rite of passage just as surely as a bar mitzvah, a train ride to college, or a first glass of beer.

The terror of turning forty is not that you are midway through life; it is that suddenly, irrevocably, you are half dead.

Hm.

I liked the play on words in a brief lead paragraph—and forgive me for losing the source—which goes: "FLENSBURG, WEST GERMANY—In a plain-brown-wrapper of a building in an industrial suburb, with all the exoticism of a forklift truck, sits what is probably the world's largest sex business."

Of all those negative reviews about the swiftly-closed stage version of *Lolita*, I perked most at John Simon's. Actors and playwrights must loathe him, but he sure has a way with words:

Vladimir Nabokov's *Lolita* was not so much adapted as debased to the stage by Edward Albee. How do I reprehend it? Let me count the ways.

I won't go on. Rest assured, it's a critical diatribe with words like "ignoramus" and "vulgarian" and "hack."

Better to end on a happy note, the lead by Adolph Green in *American Film:*

I love Fred Astaire.

News and feature leads

The UPI story began this way under a Boston dateline:

> Divers searching the murky Atlantic for the treasure of the Andrea Doria, the Italian luxury liner that sank 25 years ago, today found one of two safes believed to contain more than $1 million in jewels and valuables.
>
> It was not clear who can legally lay claim to the booty.
>
> "The first safe has been reached," said Lillian Pickard, a spokesman in New York for the organizer of the Doria expedition, Peter Gimbel. "They're very excited."

A typical news lead to a typical news story of a not-so-typical news item. The journalistic Ws and the H are supplied, at least sort of. Who: divers. What: discovery of the safe. Where: the murky Atlantic. When: today. Why: (implied) because of jewelry and valuables. How: (implied) by diving.

A reader who wants his information quickly, rather painlessly, and briefly can get it. Even without going further, he has the basics of the story which in succeeding paragraphs are elaborated on.

That's fine for a lot of stories. Sufficient. Enough.

But there are times, occasions, situations which call for more. And even the Andrea Doria story benefits from another approach. On the same day that the UPI version ran cross-country, the *New York Times* ran its own, the work of reporter Richard Severo. Note how he began his story:

> They have lost more than four days of precious diving time because of punishing high seas, with waves reaching 15 feet. They have had to dig through tons of debris, far more than they thought they would encounter. And now, as they are running out of time, the treasure hunters' major objective still remains inaccessible.
>
> But 29 days and one tropical storm after they

reached the spot where the Andrea Doria sank 200 feet to the ocean bottom 25 years ago, an expedition of weary deep-sea divers led by Peter Gimbel reported that they had found one of the ship's two safes and were preparing to bring it to the surface.

> The safes, rumored to contain more than $1 million in cash and jewelry, are believed to be buried in the rubble of the first-class foyer of the Italian luxury liner.

We're getting the story a bit more slowly here, not quickly enough perhaps for the reader who just wants the facts, unadorned. But we're gaining information, too, in the form of detail. And we're gaining atmosphere.

And that's fine for a lot of stories, better, in fact.

You should determine whether the material you have is more suitably done in straight news style or in feature form, or whether—indeed—the story lends itself to both sorts of treatment: a basic news item plus an elaborating feature.

The approval for marketing of a new drug, for instance, lends itself to news treatment: name of drug, some details of its uses, the when and wheres and hows of marketing. The event lends itself to feature treatment, too: the story of the research team through trials and tribulations.

Or let's say you open a new corporate headquarters. Of course, you can cover it in news fashion. And just as of course, you can give various feature treatments to the headquarters itself, to the inaugural event, to the people who'll be in charge of various sections of the headquarters or happenings within it.

The best approach depends on the story and your audience. It also depends on what else is in your issue and how you're treating that other material because the best publication offers variety to its readers. To do everything the same way is to assure boring the readership.

So consider offering the spice of variations.

It makes your life as a writer livelier, and it certainly does that for your reader. Good objectives, both.

'I read the news today (oh boy)'

Futurist Alvin Toffler writes in his latest tome, *The Third Wave:*

> As change accelerates in society, it forces a parallel acceleration within us. New information reaches us, and we are forced to revise our image file continuously at a faster and faster rate. . . .

> This speed-up of image processing inside us means that images grow more and more temporary. Throwaway art, one-shot sitcoms, Polaroid snapshots, Xerox copies, and disposable graphics pop up and vanish. Ideas, beliefs and attitudes skyrocket into consciousness, are challenged, defied and suddenly fade into nowhere. Scientific and psychological theories are overthrown and superseded daily. Ideologies crack. Celebrities pirouette fleetingly across our awareness. It is difficult to make sense of this swirling phantasmagoria, to understand exactly how the image-making process is changing.

One can argue about Toffler's tendency to overstate through compression of ideas and images, but he makes a point, and a valid one, which we as writers should bear in mind.

The press of life has become such that we are hard-pressed to keep up, to assimilate, to react. We are easily wearied and sometimes overwhelmed by the ever increasing impulses of sound and sight that come at us, blipping into our consciousness, begging for our response. Like rakes emptied of spirit and drained by excess, we are dulled by communicative overstimulation. Too much comes at us from too many sources in too many ways.

Result: information seeping into the brain but briefly, then escaping our memory, or information rejected because all our circuits are busy.

All of which is to say that what Toffler suggests is happening to us makes itself felt in the way readers respond to what we write.

It takes more for them to respond, more from us as writers. We cannot reach our public as easily as before. We have to shout or whisper. We have to entice. And that does not mean we should play games with our readers, trick them. Certainly not. But we must seek in every way to say what we have to say with force, with verve, with life, with brio, with that extra twist of creativity which attracts even amidst the drone of sound, sound, sound, words, words, words.

As with the *strong quote.* Pranay Gupte in the *New York Times* writes of the family of Achmat Hassan in Baghdad, and of his children, all four years or younger, and of his wife. Says Gupte of the youngsters, "They do not fully understand that their father will not be coming home anymore." And then the writer quotes a member of the family, the dead man's sister: "We are told he died a martyr. Martyr for what? How many more martyrs before we can have peace again?"

That's a quote likely to cause response.

An extra *twist of creativity which attracts.* Like the analogy which Robert Solomon provided in *Fortune* recently in the "Business Roundup," when he discusses oil shock. ". . .the OPEC hikes," he writes, "have acted as a sort of giant world-wide sales tax, raising prices and draining off purchasing power that would have been available for other goods and services."

A complex matter somewhat simplified.

And one can do it with *statistics,* too. Rodale Press of Emmaus, Pennsylvania, has done so in an advertisement called "The Losing of America": "The United States will lose 26 square miles of its land today. It will lose another 26 square miles tomorrow, and every day this year. But not to a foreign power. We are giving up our land to the ravenous demands of an unrealistic food system." The remainder of the ad explains and argues. Whether the statistic and attendant view reflect accuracy I do not know. But I do know that I paid attention.

As I did when our State Department divided the $24 billion demanded by the Iranian government by 52, which translated into $460 million per hostage.

I was impressed by *narrative,* too, usually an attention-getter if well handled. This sample comes from the mind of Howard Blum in one of a series of articles prepared for the *New York Times* on arson. Here's his provocative, evocative lead:

> The holes in the ceiling of apartment 4D had been drilled the night before. Tonight's work would be easy. But as Luis Ayala walked up the dimly lit stairwell of 2031 Seventh Avenue in Harlem,

carrying a ladder and a black bag filled with rags and a can of kerosene, he stumbled in the darkness. The bag fell open onto the tiled floor, and the sound of the kerosene can rang through the empty hallway.

In a moment, tenants were peering through apartment-door peepholes. The intruder's ladder and the red kerosene can immediately announced to the residents what was planned for the building that night: it would be set afire.

Though Luis Ayala was a small man, no one tried to stop him. Within half an hour flames were rushing through the holes he had bored in the top-floor apartment's ceiling and eating away at the roof.

Those flames, just two years ago, began a chain of events that ended in the exposing of the largest arson-for-profit ring ever uncovered in the United States.

At times of trouble journalists, their adrenalin pumping, seem to exude excitement in their words. The shooting of John Lennon brought much writing to cause us to pause. Each of you, I'm sure, found an article somewhere that perked your mind and especially touched your emotions. Let us share here three leads, by Jay Cocks in *Time,* Allan Mayer in *Newsweek,* and Pete Hamill in *New York.*

Cocks begins this way:

Just a voice out of the American night. "Mr. Lennon." He started to turn around. There is no knowing whether John Lennon saw, for what would have been the second time that day, the young man in the black raincoat stepping out of the shadows. The first shot hit him that fast, through the chest. There were at least three others.

Not that night, or the next day, but a little later, after the terror ebbed and the grief could be managed, Lennon's wife, Yoko Ono, took their five-year-old son Sean to the spot in the apartment courtyard where she had seen his father murdered. She had already shown Sean a newspaper with his father's picture on the front page. She tried to do what everyone else has done since that Monday night. She tried to explain.

Like everyone else, too, the boy asked simple questions to which there would never be simple or

satisfactory answers. If, as was being said, the man liked his father so much, why did he shoot him? His mother explained: "He was probably a confused person." Not good enough. Better to know, Sean Lennon said, if he was confused or really meant to kill. His mother said that was up to the courts to decide, and Sean wanted to know which courts she was talking about: tennis or basketball? Then Sean cried, and he also said, "Now Daddy is part of God. I guess when you die you become much more bigger because you're part of everything."

The *Newsweek* approach:

Come together, he had once asked them in a song, and now they came, tens of thousands of them, to share their grief and shock at the news. John Lennon, once the cheeky wit and sardonic soul of the Beatles, whose music had touched a generation and enchanted the world, had been slain on his doorstep by a confused, suicidal young man who had apparently idolized him. Along New York's Central Park West and West 72nd Street, in front of the building where Lennon had lived and died, they stood for hours in tearful vigil, looking to each other and his music for comfort. The scene was repeated in Dallas's Lee Park, at San Francisco's Marina Green, on the Boston Common and in countless other gathering places around the country and the world. Young and old, black and white, they lit candles and softly sang his songs. "All you need is love," they chanted in the rain. "Love is all you need."

And Pete Hamill went to the source, Lennon himself, for his inspiration:

1. I READ THE NEWS TODAY
(OH BOY)
Well nobody came to bug us,
Hustle us or shove us
So we decided to make it our home
If the Man wants to shove us out
We gonna jump and shout
The Statue of Liberty said, "Come!"
New York City. . .New York City. . . .
New York City. . .
Que pasa, New York?
Que pasa, New York?
—John Lennon, 1972

The news arrived like a fragment of some

forgotten ritual. First a flash on television, interrupting the tail end of a football game. Then the telephones ringing, back and forth across the city, and then another bulletin, with more details, and then more phone calls from around the country, from friends, from kids with stunned voices, and then the dials being flipped from channel to channel while WINS played on the radio. And yes: It was true. Yes: Somebody had murdered John Lennon.

And because it was John Lennon, and because it was a man with a gun, we fell back into the ritual. If you were there for the sixties, the ritual was part of your life. You went through it for John F. Kennedy and for Martin Luther King, for Malcolm X and for Robert Kennedy. The earth shook, and then grief was slowly handled by plunging into newspapers and television shows. We knew there would be days of cliche-ridden expressions of shock from the politicians; tearful

shots of mourning crowds; obscene invasions of the privacy of The Widow; calls for gun control; apocalyptic declarations about the sickness of America; and then, finally, the orgy over, everybody would go on with their lives.

Except. . .this time there was a difference. *Somebody murdered John Lennon.* Not a politician. Not a man whose abstract ideas could send people to wars, or bring them home; not someone who could marshal millions of human beings in the name of justice; not some actor on the stage of history. This time, someone had crawled out of a dark place, lifted a gun, and killed an artist. This was something new.

Three versions. Three thoughts. Three approaches. Compare. Contrast. But each surely gains attention. And that is the writer's job, ever more so.

Show vs tell

When you can manage it—and the story benefits from such treatment—strive for a you-are-there approach. Give the reader a feeling that an experience is being shared.

That he's deep sea diving or in an inner city school, that she's watching earth art being created in the Mojave Desert or telechtronic experiments carried out in some lab-for-the-future.

It's a matter of closeness versus distance, of nouns and verbs versus adjectives, of active versus passive tense, of things seemingly happening now versus then. It's a matter of show versus tell.

Tell is having a writer say that a seashore vacation is great and relaxing and bracing and refreshing. Show is having a writer say, "The stillness hugs you, holds you in serene comfort, caresses emotional aches and mental pains out of you. The light comes all in twinkles, up above from myriads of stars, around us from the now-and-then of fireflies. There is the swish-swish ever so soft of an almost surfless sea."

It's the writer's way of saying, "Look, I'm sorry you haven't been to the seashore, but let me take you there through my experiences, and then maybe you'll be more inclined to go yourself, although even if not, you can measure more fully what it is like."

Something normal or average can turn special. Something special or different can turn memorable. Something memorable or significant can turn unforgettable.

Nicholas Von Hoffman, reporting back from Mississippi during the 1964 summer of civil rights struggle for the Chicago *Daily News*:

Devil's dust, the little wind-stirred geysers of dry earth that blow up between the rows of cotton plants, puff here and there across the fields.

Two Negro women walk by the side of the highway. Their parasols protect them from the sun, which even now in the early morning has laid down its heat over the Mississippi Delta.

The blues and reds of the women's cotton dresses are vivid. The orange umbrella atop the tractor moving down the rows of cotton plants is unfaded in the sun's summer light.

This Mississippi sun does not bleach. It brings out color and magnifies detail so that no man can mistake another.

The lean men of Mississippi are unmistakable. They pause at the gasoline pumps in front of roadside general stores, their lifeless eyes full of suspicion, forcing your own to glance downward as you get out of your car.

In this summer the stranger is the enemy, and the men of Mississippi wait and watch for him.

Yes, it is as if we were there, sharing the experience. The words have been so carefully considered and crafted. There's no waste. Each word contributes to re-create a scene, and—as the old CBS television series used to put it—"You are there." That's show.

Timothy Crouse in his *The Boys on the Bus* takes us on an election campaign. He takes us right along. The opening goes:

June 1—five days before the California primary. A grey dawn was fighting its way through the orange curtain in the Wilshire Hyatt House Hotel in Los Angeles, where George McGovern was encamped with his wife, his staff, and the press assigned to cover his snowballing campaign.

While reporters still snored like Hessians in a hundred beds throughout the hotel, the McGovern munchkins were at work, plying the halls, slipping the long legal-sized handouts through the cracks under the door of each room. According to one of these handouts, the Baptist Ministers' Union of Oakland had decided after "prayerful and careful deliberation" to endorse Senator McGovern. . . .

At 6:45 the phone on the bed table rang, and a sweet, chipper voice announced: "Good morning, Mr. Crouse. It's six forty-five. The press bus leaves in forty-five minutes from the front of the hotel.". . .

The media heavies were rolling over, stumbling to the bathroom, and tripping over the handouts.

We're getting our faculties together right along with them, cleaning up, dressing, getting ready to catch that bus. And that's show.

"The village of Holcomb stands on the high wheat plains of western Kansas," writes Truman Capote to open *In Cold Blood:*

. . .a lonesome area that other Kansans call "out there." Some seventy miles east of the Colorado border, the countryside, with its hard blue skies and desert-clear air, has an atmosphere that is rather more Far West than Middle West. The local accent is barbed with prairie twang, a ranch-hand nasalness, and the men, many of them, wear narrow frontier trousers, Stetsons, and high-heeled boots with pointed toes. The land is flat, and the views are awesomely extensive; horses, herds of cattle, a white cluster of grain elevators rising as gracefully as Greek temples are visible long before a traveler reaches them.

Here's a sense of place, a setting of mood. The feel of the town and the folks who inhabit it emanate from the type, from the paper. And that's show.

"How Goliath, Typecast to Lose, Finally Didn't" was the title for Jeremy Larner's profile of Wilt Chamberlain in *Life*:

The big man lets his jaw fall slack. He throws his head back with a big-toothed grimace. He holds his arms out like railroad gates, enormous palms upturned to heaven. Then he shambles up the floor, wincing and shaking his head, shooting his hands down in disgust, finally wrapping them on his hips as he goes on wincing and shambling and shaking.

As if to say: How long, O Lord, must this go on? As if to say: *Just what I expected!*

And the fans howl and scream abuse—in every city but Philadelphia—because the big man is Wilt Chamberlain, who has just had a foul called on him, or watched a teammate botch a play, or learned that he will have to shoot a free throw.

Detail gives us a sense of actually watching rather than merely reading. And that's show.

Yes, detail as Paul Theroux provides continuously in *The Great Railway Bazaar*, his account of a trip by trains through Asia. Just outside London, as his adventure begins, he noted:

The sky was old. Schoolboys in dark blue blazers, carrying cricket bats and school bags, their socks falling down, were smirking on the platform at Tonbridge. We raced by them, taking their smirks away.

And Mari Sandoz recalls snakes in *Old Jules Country,* one snake particularly, the rattler that bit her father:

I stood inside the door and looked at Father's swelling arm, his puffed, purpled hand and the black-crusted wound over most of the back of it. He was quiet, his face pale and still as plaster above the heavy beard, his breath wheezing. . . .

By the time Pete was back with about an inch of brown liquid in a tall bottle, the arm was blackening to the shoulder and the swelling spreading to the chest. Father gulped the whisky with difficulty. "It's not enough," he said and sank back hopelessly. "Get me home. I want to die at home."

It gets worse before it gets better. He doesn't die. A scene brought close, gruesomely so. And that's show.

You can find samples of your own if you look for them. You can *create* samples of your own if you care to.

No, not every story should be handled this way. Oft times to tell is more than enough and much more appropriate. But, on the other hand, who's to say that an excursion into truck maintenance should lack the elements of action and description and personality that make the more consumer-oriented work of Capote and Crouse so fascinating to read? Who's to say that health care or toy merchandising or banking should get duller treatment than a journey on the Orient Express or to the Mississippi Delta?

The writer's job, after all, is to engage the reader. What does? Show more than tell, that's what.

Narrative gives both event and meaning

Perusal of *A Treasury of Great Reporting* reminds one that journalists have long treasured the narrative, not only to recount an event but also to illustrate a point. Narratives make good reading.

Consumer-oriented publications use them heavily. Their writers are attuned to the reading habits of those who purchase the local newspaper, the regional magazine, the special interest publication. Those habits favor story telling.

The business/trade press has been slower picking up the technique, perhaps seeking to convince itself that business/trade readers are too serious for what, after all, is the province and property and product of the fiction writer.

Well, all that's changing. The savvy business/trade editor wants to reach his readership more easily and more tellingly. He knows the carefully used narrative can help. It gains attention. It holds attention. It calls attention to an issue.

As did a writer for *Dun's Review* in the lead to "What's a Diamond Really Worth?"

When swank specialty store Neiman-Marcus sold a $120,000 diamond to a Florida resident seven years ago, the store was confident of the stone's D-Flawless rating, the highest attainable. After all, the ten-carat stone carried the industry pedigree: a certificate from the Gemological Institute of America, a New York-based nonprofit industry association that has been the preeminent grader of diamonds for the past twenty-five years.

But the trusting buyer was shocked when, several years later, he decided to sell the same diamond. The GIA took a second look, and downgraded the stone to an "E." The one-grade difference translated into twenty-four thousand dollars in the stone's value, and in a lawsuit decided this spring, Neiman-Marcus was ordered to pay damages for the difference. GIA's standard disclaimers of responsibility for such losses freed the institute of any liability.

The article then follows with a brief paragraph that takes the reader into the heart of the subject matter: "The Neiman-Marcus episode points up one of the hazards of investing in diamonds: how can a person be sure he is getting what he has paid for?" A narrative in incident form to exemplify a problem. An effective method.

Amanda Bennett uses the narrative as structure for her entire *Wall Street Journal* story on the human model business at trade shows. She decided to be one and tells of her experiences, beginning this way:

I have two blisters on each foot. My shoulders are bare and the drafty hall is freezing, yet I'm sweating with anxiety. Once again, I've forgotten my memorized lines. At my side, a man making disgusting kissing sounds is trying to attract my attention.

Welcome to the exciting, glamorous world of auto-show modeling.

It's evocative, a present-tense, it-seems-to-be-happening-now approach to a business practice of our day. And nothing could get the reader closer to an understanding of that practice than a first person experience, a narrative, a true story.

A narrative can set the scene, too, directing a reader into a world of feeling. William Serrin approached his *New York Times* story, "A Certainty in Uncertain Times: Football in the Fall," that way:

McDonald, Ohio—High, high in the black night, the football tumbled, and then it began to fall, and so it had begun, the game that was so important to the stout-hearted McDonald players, to students, to parents, the game that was the most important thing of all on this Friday night, in October, in Ohio.

They have not changed, these shining fall nights of youth when the playing fields are alight, the fans cheer, and the bands play.

Serrin departs from his story to express how the game in Ohio reflects games and mood all over the land. So sensitively he states: "The young men still wear their jerseys to school on game day. They still sit dourly at the pep rallies, and the pep bands play and the girls watch the players and the players know the girls are watching them. The hard-eyed coaches still exhort their men not to quit, to do their best. The girls still curl their hair just so, and they smell so fresh. And the bandsmen high-step down the field, and their tassels, in school colors, bounce on their white shiny boots. Friday night," concludes Serrin, "is high school football night for much of America."

In another *Times* story, John Kifner uses the incidental narrative to suggest a mood and reality of quite another sort:

Beirut, Lebanon—When Mounir Fatha's blue Fiat turned the corner, its path was blocked by another car coming the wrong way up the narrow, one-way street. It was not an uncommon occurrence in this battered, anarchic city, where any semblance of traffic rules has long been forgotten. What followed, however, touched off a 10-hour battle in which rival leftist militiamen hurled rockets, mortars and heavy machine-gun fire at each other through the heart of western Beirut's main shopping district.

Neither car would give way. Instead, the two drivers got out and exchanged harsh words. The disagreement ended in gunfire. The driver of the second car—a member of the National Syrian Social Party, one of Beirut's 17 leftist militia groups—pulled out a pistol and shot Mr. Fatha and his driver to death.

Newsweek in its special issue on "A Day to Remember" utilized two brief narratives to get the discussion underway:

They rode one last time through the blacked-out streets of Teheran in a curtailed white bus and slipped into Mehrabad Airport by a sealed-off back gate. They spilled out onto the moonlit tarmac, looking dazed and lank-haired in their motley of denim, sandals and ill-fitting Iranian fatigues. They endured one last torment between them and the waiting Air Algerie 727—a forced march past a gauntlet of militants raining kicks and curses on them. And then they were aboard, the runway lights blazed on, and the jet roared aloft bearing the 52 hostage Americans on their long night's journey into day.

He stood at almost precisely that moment on the West Front of the Capitol, looking down over a vista of white monuments to Washington, Jefferson and Lincoln agleam in the warming sunlight. He had placed his hand on a crumbling family Bible and been sworn as the 40th President of the United States, to the thud-thudding of howitzers and the swell of patriotic hymns. And now, with his predecessor sitting by in defeat, it was his turn to summon the nation to believe once again in itself and its capacity for great deeds. "And after all," said Ronald Reagan, his voice thick with emotion, "why shouldn't we believe that? We are Americans."

"It was Day 444 and Day One come together in rare historic symmetry" went on the article.

Whether it is something nationally momentous or it involves the development of an unusual housing project, the narrative can serve to show readers both event and meaning, at once, pithily, even powerfully.

More on narratives

The problem of discipline in the public schools, let's say, can be covered through a series of interviews, with teachers, with students, with school administrators, with parents and educational philosophers. And certainly a writer seeking to do a story on that subject would or should seek out these sources of information.

The problem could be told through statistics, and the thoughtful writer will gather those statistics that show change and extent.

The problem could be handled through overview, through examples that explain what goes on in Philadelphia schools and Atlanta schools and Seattle schools and Keokuk schools. The information-gathering writer should get such material because at the very least it gives him context.

The problem also could be unfolded narratively, through the eyes and ears, the experiences and pains of one teacher, his or her day on the job. The combative atmosphere in the classroom, the reprimands and warnings, the trips down to the principal's office, the disruptions from lessons, the monitor duty in the lunchroom, the rowdiness at assembly, the despair of the teacher, the dejection of those students who want to learn.

In that running narrative—perhaps interrupted occasionally by a telling statistic or a powerful quote from an authority—the situation we face nationally could be ventilated. And silently, without polemics, the case for smaller classes or more teachers or different divisions or altered educational approaches or student-run class governance can be argued.

Not that you would always want to do it that way. But it's an option. And it's a highly effective one. Think of what interests you, what makes you perk. It's likely to be a story. It's likely to be an account—told or written or shown—of human activity. We are beguiled or appalled by what people do to themselves and each other, more so than by things or opinions.

All those sociological tomes on poverty and deprivation pale when held against Oscar Lewis' *The Children of Sanchez,* his "autobiography of a Mexican family." "Irela didn't get pregnant," he writes, just to give you a sample chosen at random (I happened to open the book to page 150),

but anyway she went to live in Donato's mother's house. He worked in a bakery and spent the little he earned on shoes and dresses for Irela. She was pretty and he was ugly and the truth was, they didn't make a nice couple. She didn't pay attention to him at all. She didn't care whether he had anything to eat or wear, and let her mother-in-law do all the work. Donato was one of those men who had the habit of bringing his friends home and Irela didn't like to stay there. So she came over to talk to me for hours. I was going with Crispin and wanted to know as much as possible about what men do, so I asked her lots of questions.

And on page 474:

Baltasar had been coming home very late, or not at all. I warned him that it was dangerous for him to be out alone when he was drunk, but he thinks it's like in Acapulco. The other night a bunch of boys. . .all rebels without cause. . .chased him and he barely escaped. I told him that if anything happened to him, his relatives would come and blame me. They would come and chew me up alive because that's the way his race of people is. But he doesn't think of that. He says all I do is scold and get angry, that all I want is to keep him tied up at home.

Baltasar stayed away for two days. When he came in, I handed him the prescription. "Take this," I said, "and ask the Pig for money to buy it because the doctor told me it was urgent." He was surprised that I didn't yell at him and he tried to embrace me. All I said was, "Stop bothering me. Here I am with my daughters, and you come molesting me. Who told you to come? What devil brought you? The street is your home!"

Lewis uses running narratives based on his interviews with various members of the family. And as they unfold, we learn what makes people and families go on despite the atmosphere that surrounds them. "The Sociology of a Mexican Family" would get the scrutiny of two dozen scholars scattered round about the world, plus maybe a class or two where the teacher has assigned it as must reading. *The Children of Sanchez* becomes avid reading for thousands of people every year. The book is a narrative, but within the story are exposition and argumentation. We find out what it's all about, and within our minds we determine what's right and what's wrong and who's to blame.

It really does work. Narrative can work for you.

The Wall Street Journal makes use of narratives frequently. Its best articles usually run in columns one and four on the front page, and more often than not they're narrative pieces. But you know when they run in the *Journal,* there's got to be a point. And so, when a reporter takes us to the scene of a five-alarm fire in a Manhattan skyscraper, he does so to show—through the men's combat with that blaze—what we should consider about safety and danger as we go to work or go to our apartment in some big city highrise, if such we do.

So Sally Quinn did a while back in the Washington *Post*'s Style section when recounting her tenth reunion at Smith College. But hers were two narratives within one story, the first devoted to the reunion, the second to memories of back then. She moved back and forth between the recent yesterday and long-ago yesterdays. And the result was to witness not only her reunion but all reunions, and even more important to understand through her thoughtful reflections all those back-of-the-mind tugs about age creeping up on us and friends dropping away from us and life losing meaning or gaining new ones.

So a former student of mine, Andrew Wolfson, did in a cover piece for the Chicago *Tribune* magazine when he attempted—quite successfully—to reveal the problems of medical interning through the story of one woman intern at one hospital during one 33-hour marathon shift. He stopped the narrative from time to time to let another intern talk about weariness or to let a hospital administrator discuss understaffing and overwork. But the article runs on a narrative track. And we learn what it's like to be an intern, to treat patients that get well and patients that die.

It's the show versus tell technique. The writers are taking us to the scene, permitting us to experience what they have observed first hand.

John Leonard's "Private Lives" pieces in the *New York Times* often are narratives meant to do what-we-all-are-about duty. "Surprise!" began one of his columns:

It was a birthday party, and we therefore behaved like trombones, and the victim was pleased, and the tears fell like dimes, and I looked at the ceiling, which is where I always look when the spy business takes me to the vital and dangerous Upper West Side, as if to accommodate eagles or bats. And yet the people who live under these high ceilings do not, on the whole, seem bigger than the people who live elsewhere in New York, perhaps because they eat so much Chinese food. . . .

The narrative continues, until he writes:

I was pleased that the victim was pleased by the surprise birthday party. In my experience, surprises are as dangerous as birthdays, radical ideas and the Upper West Side. The sort of person who likes a surprise party at his or her expense is also the sort of person likely to have guessed or expected that one was in the works, whereas the sort of person who is genuinely surprised by a party, like a bomb, will probably fear it, or hate birthdays, or get nosebleeds from high ceilings.

Leonard takes us through the party, as filtered through his inventive mind, of course. But his aim is not just to tell what happened because who really cares about what happens at a birthday party at which virtually nothing happens to guests we cannot care about and a birthday lady we're never going to meet? Toward the conclusion, he writes:

I counted the number of trombones who knew my secrets. It was scary. There wasn't a mirror or a heart I could look into. I didn't like my image. No wonder the ceilings are high. There would be no room otherwise for all the guilt to breathe. . .

He had something to say about casual relationships and impersonality and ties that are not bound except by empty conventions. The story of that birthday party was his way of doing so.

You can write of your hangups that way. You also can reveal what really happened at a conference, skipping reportage of speeches given and papers published, instead concentrating on what one conventioneer did hour upon hour.

The narrative can reach to the heart of things. And people.

Power of detail

Don't say the lady is a moderate smoker if you know she puffs through a dozen cigarettes a day. Don't say the boy is above average in height for his age if you know he's 5'11'' at age 11. Don't say dog if you know it's a dachshund.

Be specific. Provide the detail that shows your reader how observant you are and gives the reader an insight which the generality can never give.

I enjoyed a piece by Roger Simon of the Chicago *Sun-Times* a few years back about a visitor to the city:

A tourist came to the United States this week and stopped off in Chicago to buy a few trinkets to remind him of his visit.

Funny thing, though, he didn't buy any satin pillows that said "My Kind of Town!" or ceramic ashtrays in the shape of Mayor Daley's head. And he didn't take the things home in a J.C. Penney's shopping bag, either.

Instead, this particular visitor stocked up on a few items, went to the Circle Airfreight Corp. near O'Hare Airport and had it hire a Boeing 747 cargo jet for $194,500.

The tourist was the Sultan of Oman, Qabus bin Said (he thinks your name sounds funny, too) and, to be fair, he needed a Boeing 747 for his shopping spree. The knickknacks he purchased included:

* Six Cadillac Sevilles.
* A Cadillac Eldorado.
* Six Mercedes-Benz sedans.
* A 25-foot, cigar-shaped speedboat.
* A Chevy truck.
* A Targa Porsche.
* A Porsche 911-S.
* A hundred women's Samsonite suitcases.
* Sixteen refrigerators from Polk Bros.
* A gas range from Polk Bros.
* Twenty-four thousand pounds of automotive tools.
* Three grapefruit trees.
* Two Lazy Boy reclining chairs.

There's really no story here without the details, the specifics. The price of the cargo jet, the fact that it's a 747, the list of items from cigar-shaped speedboat to grapefruit trees. Simon has made a delightful story out of something very close to a no-story. The above is merely an excerpt. It makes one want to read on.

"October is the richest of the seasons," writes Thomas Wolfe in *Of Time and the River.* "The fields are cut, the granaries are full, the bins are loaded to the brim with fatness, and from the cider-press the rich brown oozings of the York Imperials run. The bee bores to the belly of the yellowed grape, the fly gets old and fat and blue, he buzzes loud, crawls slow, creeps heavily to death on sill and ceiling, the sun goes down in blood and pollen across the bronzed and mown fields of old October."

There's much more about October, and it all depends on how closely Wolfe has looked at the season and thought about it and remembered it. The color and feel are in the details. Without details, there'd be nothing.

On a much more earthy level of language use, yet making the same point, is the work of Charles Price in a profile for *Golf Magazine* of the legendary Bobby Jones. Price might merely have said that Jones was an almost flawless golfer and a great competitor and a nice human being. But then, what really would he have said? The adjectives are emptily general. He's opted for meatier nouns and verbs:

Jones so devastated the opposition with his arrogance toward par and his disrespect for the record books that he could have been the most despised golfer of his day. Actually, he was the most admired and genuinely liked. No one before or since him has played the game with more modesty, thoughtfulness and integrity. On the night before his Sunday playoff with Al Espinosa for the 1929 Open at Winged Foot, Jones, unknown to Espinosa, requested that the officials postpone the starting time for an hour so that Espinosa might have time to attend Mass. At four national championships, Jones called penalty strokes on himself for minor breaches of the rules. In the 1925 U.S. Open at Worcester, Massachusetts, he insisted on penalizing himself a stroke when his ball accidentally moved slightly in the rough when the blade of his iron touched the turf. No one else possibly could have seen the ball move, and the officials poo-poohed the incident. But Jones insisted. That stroke cost him the title, which he lost in a playoff with Willie MacFarlane, and eventually prevented him from becoming the only man ever to win five U.S. Opens. When Jones was praised for throwing the book at himself, he became indignant. "There is only one way to play the game," he said. "You might as well praise a man for not robbing a bank."

There's the man. Details captured him.

That extra word, the special fact can lift your story out of the commonplace. Take William Serrin's beginning to this story with a Coalport, Pennsylvania, dateline:

What he would not forget, after he had left the hospital where she lay, still in her sweatshirt and long underwear and coveralls, on an emergency room cart, was that there was nothing to suggest she was dead.

The only marks he could see were a small bump and a cut on her left temple. A trickle of blood from the cut matted a bit of her hair. It was like a scrape from striking a car door or a kitchen cabinet. She looked as she did when she was alive.

There was one other thing. Her hands.

Her face, like all coal miners' faces, was black with coal. But her hands had been covered with gloves. And, as she lay on the hospital cart, the gloves removed, her hands were as white as snow.

And the coroner came and pronounced her dead.

The next day the autopsy was performed, and the undertaker took her body to a small, one-story, brick funeral home on Main Street in this small, dark town, stuck into a long hollow between two steep, wooded ridges. They laid her out there. . . .

And then we find out about Marilyn McCusker, who had gone to court to win the right to work in the mines and then became the first woman killed in an underground mine in this country. The detail in Serrin's writing—of how she looked, all the way down to those hands "white as snow"—create a mood of sadness that makes the story something to be remembered.

And that's the power of detail. Look for that specific. Use it.

Description

The eminent biologist Thomas Huxley pressed years ago—unsuccessfully I might add—for public schools in England to concentrate on the teaching of art in the very primary grades and then in continuation throughout a youngster's education.

Not, he emphasized, to produce more artists, of which there already were too many, he concluded, or to produce more masterpieces, which would be an unlikely by-product, but to sharpen the human faculty for observation.

"I do not think its [art's] value can be exaggerated," he said, "because it gives you the means of training the young in attention and accuracy, in which all mankind are more deficient than in any other mental quality whatever."

"Accurate perception," he argued, is the first step to education, to the scientist, and, of course, to the writer—"the ability to see clearly, to describe the world in which he finds himself."

People's deficiency can be compensated for if writers are observant, accurately so and effectively so.

Accurate and effective observation is the most critical aspect of description. Accuracy depends on the writer's carefulness to put in the right words what he has experienced. Effectiveness depends on the writer's sincerity, not permitting words to escape control, not to overwrite but to be oneself.

Of course, the writer filters that observed material through the imagination. And that makes even common things special.

As the New York *Times* editorial writer put it: "Your head feels as though a taxidermist has been at it: nothing between your ears but stuffing. Your eyes are small, red and runny; your nose is large, red and runny; and your sneezes rock the room. 'Nobody ever died of hay fever,' your friends say. A lot they know."

As those fourth graders did some years ago when their teacher asked them to complete the sentence, "Let's be as quiet as. . ." They wrote of a leaf turning colors, a feather falling from a bird, an uninhabited creek, time passing, a plant growing, an old hat sitting in the attic, the first star coming out, the sun coming up in the morning, a tissue being crumpled, a wink of the eye, children sleeping, an ant while it is walking, when you pray, a butterfly flying, a pumpkin lit up, a leaf falling, a clock going through time.

Good thinking resulting in good similes which can result in good description, if not overused. And speaking of overuse in description, don't make too much of metaphors or figures of speech or adjectives or seeing (when one also can touch and hear and smell and taste).

The best description quite often is the most simply written, but where the words have been filtered through the writer's thoughts and emerged as something from life yet bigger than life, as a moment frozen in time yet a moment for all time.

William K. Stevens managed that after witnessing the return of the 52 Americans held hostage 444 days by the Iranians:

At first, for most of America, the drama's penultimate chapter was like a silent movie filmed at a distance.

Freedom One materialized as a white dot against the pale-blue sky to the east, grew rapidly into a ghostly gray jetliner that flew quickly over the heads of the sparse crowd that had somehow gotten into Stewart International Airport, then disappeared behind the winter-brown hills of the Hudson Valley. Suddenly it was back, swooping low in the other direction, out of the midafternoon sun and the January chill, touching down and taxiing slowly to a stop.

Making its final maneuvers, the big jet rolled onto a concrete apron in the valley between two long, narrow, snow-patched hillsides, one crowned by the control tower draped in yellow, the other carpeted by human beings there to record or simply to appreciate the moment.

The plane stopped. Its doors opened, and there emerged a series of little black dots, all that was visible at a distance of perhaps 2,500 yards of the homecoming, finally, of the 52 former hostages as they stepped onto a 50-foot-long golden carpet.

The sound came at last. "Eee-yows! and "Yay-ays!" and "Awrights!" erupted from the crowd of hillside watchers who, like everyone else, were kept at a distance so that the reunion of the former hostages and their families—seen as a mixture of multicolored dots at the foot of the plane—could be kept private and personal.

One could only imagine what tears and heart-thumpings, what laughter and expressions of love, what fears and misgivings must have flooded the tarmac. . .

A situation re-creatable only through description and done here with almost delicate sensitivity. Stevens, like the others, was kept distant, yet he somehow made the distance smaller, almost into a closeness. That's the mark of deft description: bringing the reader close to scene or being.

Herman Melville overcomes distance, the distance between late 20th century America and the Encantadas of Enchanted Isles in mid-19th century. Not only that, but he overwhelms our senses:

. . .behold these really wondrous tortoises—none of your schoolboy mud-turtles—but black as widow's weeds, heavy as chests of plate, with vast shells medallioned and orbed like shields, and dented and blistered like shields that have breasted a battle, shaggy, too, here and there, with dark green moss, and slimy with the spray of the sea. These mystic creatures, suddenly translated by night from unutterable solitudes to our peopled deck, affected me in a manner not easy to unfold. They seemed newly crawled forth from beneath the foundations of the world.

The writer of description searches for those words which re-create the atmosphere of the happening or creature itself. George Orwell describes a hanging:

It was in Burma, a sodden morning of the rains. A sickly light, like yellow tinfoil, was slanting over the high walls into the jail yard. We were waiting outside the condemned cells, a row of sheds fronted with double bars, like small animal cages. Each cell measured about ten feet by ten and was quite bare within except for a plank bed and a pot for drinking water. In some of them brown silent men were squatting at the inner bars, with their blankets draped around them. These were the condemned men, due to be hanged within the next week or two.

One prisoner had been brought out of his cell. He was a Hindu, a puny wisp of a man, with a shaven head and vague liquid eyes. He had a thick, sprouting mustache, absurdly too big for his body, rather like a mustache of a comic man

on the films. Six tall Indian warders were guarding him and getting him ready for the gallows. . . .

Orwell takes us step by step, moment by moment, until:

Suddenly the superintendent made up his mind. Throwing up his head he made a swift motion with his stick. "Chalo!" he shouted almost fiercely.

There was a clanking noise, and then dead silence. The prisoner had vanished, and the rope was twisting on itself. I let go of the dog, and it galloped immediately to the back of the gallows; but when it got there, it stopped short, barked, and then retreated into a corner of the yard, where it stood among the weeds, looking timorously at us.

It is almost too much to take, but it is—after all—an event recalled for us in detail and enhanced by a writer's feelings.

And so it is with description; events are made sharper, people are made bigger or smaller, sharper or nicer or meaner through the writer's reactions.

Tom Wolfe, the "New Journalism's" Mr. Adjective, considers Las Vegas:

. . .Las Vegas is the only town in the world whose skyline is made up neither of buildings, like New York, nor of trees, like Wilbraham, Massachusetts, but signs. One can look at Las Vegas from a mile away on Route 91 and see no buildings, no trees, only signs. But such signs! They tower. They revolve, they oscillate, they soar in shapes before which the existing vocabulary of art history is helpless. I can only attempt to supply names—Boomerang Modern, Palette Curvilinear, Flash Gordon Ming-Alert Spiral, McDonald's Hamburger Parabola, Mint Casino Elliptical, Miami Beach Kidney. Las Vegas' sign makers work so far out beyond the frontiers of conventional studio art that they have no names themselves for the forms they create.

A place, as it is and as it is perceived, description that has turned almost into argumentation and into philosophy.

Notice how in quieter ways two other contemporary journalists describe their subjects. First,

Joe Flaherty, as he writes about former fighter Jake La Motta in *Inside Sports:*

The La Motta you meet today hardly qualifies for a portrait in ferocity. If it weren't for his classically failed souffle of a face and the thickness of his articulate speech, you wouldn't suspect he had made his living at demolition. His weight is back to the 160-pound middleweight limit, and his manner is deferential. His hands belie their destructive force in that they are small, slim, and tapered.

"I should have been an artist, or a fag," he jokes. But the jibe has insight. They look like the hands of someone who would beat helplessly on the chest of a bully.

Only the eyes give a clue to his former life. They are so sad and placid, they almost look burned out. Twin novas which didn't survive the Big Bang, memos to some terrible past.

What a way to describe eyes (and a man). William Brashler's subject in the magazine, *Chicago*, is an old-style machine politician, slowed but far from petrified:

His face is the soft dough of age. He is 76 years old, pale, wattled, a touch of natural rouge in the cheeks. His eyes are clear but enfeebled, unable to see the flanks that he once saw so well. The fleshy eyelids droop; just above his eyebrows are patches of liver spots. Thin, light-brown hair is combed straight back from a high, lined forehead.

With certain syllables his tongue presses his upper teeth in a slight lisp, and you strain to hear him. Occasionally he lifts his hands from his lap and points a delicate and crooked finger. His hands are also soft, the hands of an old man who seldom has had the need to grasp a tool any heavier than a pencil, or a scalpel.

Yet while the flesh may be withering, the eyes seeing less, the step a bit slower, there is not a thing wrong with the mind. It still clicks and computes and machinates, and makes up for what the body is letting down. As usual, Tom Keane is not dead yet.

He asks questions knowing the answers. He supplies answers evading the questions. He jabs. He toys. He winks. The old fox is about; you may want to count the chickens in the coop.

Narrative writing, of course, depends on description. But so does all writing, at least wherever and whenever the writer seeks to *show* what he has witnessed. Description seasons writing, gives it flavor, makes the topic more memorable, that is if the writer knows how to do it well.

For that, study other writers.

For that, practice. Describe, in a phrase, the aroma of coffee. Describe, in a sentence, your entry into the darkness of a movie house. Describe, in a paragraph, a woman or man you admire. And do so without cliche.

Tough task, description.

Support

Assertions are easy. Support is more difficult.

Assertions without support lack meaning, import, impact. They're not likely to be remembered, either.

You can say Azazaz Corporation is the most progressive outfit in all of the Southwest. But unless you can provide evidence, the assertion amounts to an empty boast.

When in an article you wish to make a point, you need convincing facts to sell it. So if Azazaz has quadrupled its business while no other outfit has more than doubled its, say so. If Azazaz has its own retirement village for employees and a pension program that gives retirees the same monthly stipend they got while working, say so. If Azazaz scientists have discovered a way to cut energy consumption in half through the use of boiled seaweed, say so. If Azazaz has a working atmosphere that approximates Capri, say so.

Not only say so, but show *how* business quadrupled, *how* the retirement village operates, *how* the seaweed saves energy (and *how* the discovery was made), and *how* folks can do their office work out of doors poolside in bathing suits as long as they get that work done.

Let's take an assertive example and then support it.

Assertion: The poor press in America—how people inside and outside abuse it!

Abuse from within?

Well, one can cite dehumanizing computers and systems, cut budgets, and limited personnel rosters. We can add management's dependence on consultants who insist that the news be lightened and brightened and by all means cut short.

Yes, and front page stories about the problems of transvestites while stories about the demise of social welfare agencies get cozy inside spots. And weathermen bringing baby bears and chimps to the television news set, better to evoke yuks and giggles.

And Saturday Night Fever dance contests to seek the next John Travolta. And psychic predictions. And we spawn Cheryl Tiegs and Farrah Fawcett and one Punk Rock outfit after another. Support for an assertion, in the form of examples.

And then, as I once told the Society for

Professional Journalists:

We carry out a survey among junior and senior high school students, seeking to determine what man and what woman they view as having done the most damage in the world. The man selected was Adolf Hitler, and the woman selected was Anita Bryant.

Now, it's pretty hard to argue about Adolf Hitler; he surely ranks as villain of our century. But to put poor Anita in that category—ahead of, just for argument, Ilse Koch, the so-called bitch of Buchenwald?

Anita as most damaging. Anita also as the woman who makes you angriest. There she's paired by the youngsters with Richard Nixon.

This, of course, is the result of youngsters being bombarded with television gossip news and fan publications and celeb magazines where only certain sorts are written and spoken of.

I mean, whoever writes about Ilse Koch these days?

Surveys of total uselessness. Surveys that damage. Even when the same poll concludes that Abraham Lincoln and Eleanor Roosevelt have done the most good for the world. I admire them. But who can gauge Lincoln's values versus Gandhi's or Beethoven's or Booker T. Washington's? What valid measurements can we use to compare Mrs. Roosevelt with Madame Curie or Jane Addams?

Choices are made in pools by what people know and don't know, what's on their minds and what isn't. And to pass along such nonsense, as one magazine recently did, and as we who practice journalism seem to do more and more, is a form of abuse.

Support in lengthier form. One example, an example of statistics misused. I mixed in some more argument, as you can see. But all of it supports the assertion made of abuse from within.

Abuse from outside? Well, let me go back to my talk and take from it a narrative of a fellow who at the time had climbed part way up Chicago's Sears Tower:

The Chicago climber—a 25-year-old fanatic named Joseph Healy—had a clear purpose for his stunt.

His was a media stunt.

After he climbed to the 20th floor of the 110-story building, he descended to the eighth-floor level and secured a 30-foot banner for all to see.

The banner had a drawing of a whale. Plus words in three languages.

In Russian, "Do not kill the whales."

In Japanese, "Japan, stop whaling."

In English, "Green peace."

After he came down, and the police took him in custody, Healy told reporters that all he feared was that the wind would tear down his banner.

Why climb the Sears Tower? He told police: "If the whale is the world's biggest animal and it's dying, and the Sears is the world's tallest building"—then symbolically, it should be used. He later told the judge: "I had no recourse to my government. The only way to get my message across was to bring it to the public."

Healy did it for a cause. To get us to pay attention, to get us to believe. He took an extreme route because he knew that then the press would be there. He knew he would be heard.

Good cause? Maybe. But if for good cause, why not for bad? Why not an American fascist climbing some steel and glass scraper of the sky? And get the same press people there with cameras—and then the nut could say, "Hail Benito."

Support. A narrative in this case.

Analogies can support assertions. So can statistics and statements from experts. So can eye-witness description.

Facts support assertions. Facts carefully gathered and carefully clothed in language that attracts.

An assertion made is not an assertion sold. So make the assertion, and then sell it.

Definitions

The dictionary says imports are "merchandise or commodities or articles imported from abroad." That's a definition of little use save to a school child or someone just learning the language who comes upon the word and does not yet know its meaning.

In *Forbes* I spotted: "Maybe imports are what happens when Big Business and Big Labor get fat and happy and decide to deal with inflation by passing it on to the customer."

That's a definition with a point of view, a creative definition. It wouldn't fit every occasion, but the more expansive way of defining words provides the journalist with a useful tool for exposition.

A good definition explains.

The dictionary says a judge is "one who judges, a public official designated/appointed/elected/authorized to make decisions on questions before a court." Functional, no more.

So, Syd Harris, the clever syndicated columnist, writes: "A judge is an official who sentences a stranger he has never seen before, to a prison the judge has never visited, on the basis of a law the judge did not make, under the absurd pretext that this stranger's long and close association with other lawbreakers will somehow return him to society a better man than when he went in."

Now that teaches me something.

But you needn't always be clever to be creative in definition. When I asked the editor of an agricultural publication to define cow so that he might give food for thought to his particular kind of reader (the dictionary says cow is "the mature female of cattle or of any animal the male of which is called bull; also a domestic bovine animal regardless of sex or age"), that editor responded with this:

If God created one creature to save the starving masses of the world, surely it was the dairy cow.

Old Bossy can convert grass and pea vines and discarded ice cream cones—even nitrogen fertilizers—into nature's most complete, most life sustaining food.

And she does it with abundance, producing 10 to 20 times her body weight in milk each 10-month lactation.

This docile creature harvests her own food, replenishes the soil with her waste and furnishes her own replacement. When she eventually wears out after four or six years in the milk string, she's converted into McDonald hamburgers, Florsheim shoes, and steam bone meal for your dog food and garden.

On the millions of square miles not suited for corn and soybeans, and wheat, she can live in animal splendor.

Given the chance, this grand old dairy cow would easily nourish the world's poor and underfed.

That's definition. Useful. Meaningful. It could be the foundation for an article on the importance and the problems and the potential of dairy farming. It explains.

It also shows you needn't make argumentative use of the journalistic definition. *Forbes* and Harris do. One can enjoy their definitions or get angry at them or debate validity. The definition of cow is more an education than a possible point of contention.

Time began its story on "Cocaine: Middle Class High" with a definition, part dictionary-formal and part journalistically-free:

$C_{17}H_{21}NO_4$. A derivative of Erythroxylon coca. Otherwise known as cocaine, coke, C, snow, blow, toot, leaf, flake, freeze, happy dust, nose candy, Peruvian lady, white girl. A vegetable alkaloid derived from leaves of the coca plant. Origin: eastern slopes of the Andes mountains. Availability: Anywhere, U.S.A. Cost: $2,200 per oz., five times the price of gold.

And on the death in 1981 of philosopher-historian Will Durant, we were reminded of his definition of civilization. "Civilization," he said, "is a stream with banks." Most historians, he noted, concentrate on the stream "which is sometimes filled with blood from people killing, stealing, shouting." He preferred observing the banks where "unnoticed, people build homes, make love, raise children, sing songs, write poetry, whittle statues."

Let's try one more. An editor, the word book tells us, is "one who edits or prepares literary matter; the supervising director of a newspaper or other periodical."

What's that tell you about yourself? Not a whole lot. What's it tell the public out there about you and your work? Not a whole lot.

So, let's try a definition that tells more.

An editor creates, prestidigitates, conducts, plans, writes, promotes, designs, supervises.

An editor creates dreams. An editor educates and entertains.

An editor needs not only journalistic talent, even brilliance, but strength of personality, dependability, responsibility, diplomacy.

An editor is more interested in the process of work than in him or herself.

An editor looks at the world as a place to serve and people as beloved creatures to serve.

An editor holds little cynicism, some skepticism, and much idealism.

An editor thinks about life and seeks a philosophy for it.

An editor reads with pleasure.

An editor is open to the poetry of our existence, or some aspect of it.

An editor is aware of issues, slurps up ideas, and yearns to share them.

An editor is someone special who feels completed by that something special, that publication we call a magazine or newspaper or newsletter.

An editor *is* someone special.

A definition is something special, if used with imagination. It can enhance your exposition and thereby enhance your writing.

More on the tools of exposition to come.

Tools of exposition

It's easy to be boring while explaining something. It's better to be engaging.

Charles Kuralt is engaging.

The journalist we think of as describer and narrator of the American way often gives us glimpses of that American way through deft pieces of exposition. Analysis, for instance, to separate something whole into parts, thereby to learn what makes that something what it is or what it does:

> GREAT SALT LAKE, UTAH. What's in the Great Salt Lake? Nothing, you say. Well, that's the wrong answer. I've just learned what's in the Great Salt Lake, and it's a rather long list. Number 1: Salt. Eight billion tons of salt, worth about fifty billion dollars. Also gypsum, magnesium, lithium, sulfur, boron, and potash. Number 2: Shrimp. Cute little shrimp, pink with big black eyes. Also flies, gnats, and algae. Number 3: People, mostly swimming people. Swimmers like the Great Salt Lake. Nonswimmers are absolutely knocked out by it because they can't sink. There's no record of anybody ever having gone swimming and drowned in the Great Salt Lake. The best life preserver, they say, is a ten-pound weight tied to your feet, to keep your feet down and your head up.
>
> What else is in the Great Salt Lake? Number 4: A railroad. The solid rock-fill Southern Pacific trestle has divided the lake into two parts and two colors. The southern part is fresher and therefore bluer. Number 5: Waves.

You'll have to get the rest of the ingredients, the rest of the analysis, the take-apart of the Great Salt Lake from Mr. Kuralt's book, *Dateline America* (Harcourt Brace Jovanovich), based on his piquant reports on CBS.

Other writers analyze, too, of course. Here's another example to make sure you get the point. This one is from Hitler's minister of armaments Albert Speer, part of his testimony when he was tried for war crimes after World War Two:

> Hitler's dictatorship differed in one fundamental point from all its predecessors in history. It was the first dictatorship in the present period of modern technical development, a dictatorship which made complete use of all technical means for the domination of its own country. Through technical devices like the radio and the loud-speaker, eighty million people were deprived of independent thought. It was thereby possible to subject them to the will of one man.

Contrast (the way two things or people or events are different) and comparison (the way they're alike) can help to make expositional material clearer. Kuralt offers this item based on contrast, dateline, Lake Tahoe, California:

> That irrepressible old tourist, Mark Twain, walked up the mountains from Carson City carrying an ax and a couple of blankets to take a look at Lake Tahoe and found it worth the climb.
>
> "As it lay there," he wrote, "with the shadows of the mountains brilliantly photographed upon its still surface, I thought it must surely be the fairest picture the whole earth affords."
>
> That was 115 years ago. Today there is smog about the lake.
>
> "So singularly clear was the water," Mark Twain wrote, "that even where it was 80 feet deep, the bottom was perfectly distinct. . . .The water was not merely transparent, but dazzlingly, brilliantly so."
>
> Today brown smudges muddy the water hundreds of yards out into the lake, the runoff from the towns on shore.
>
> "Three miles away," Mark Twain wrote, "was a sawmill and some workmen, but there were not 15 other human beings throughout the wide circumference of the lake. . .We did not see a human being but ourselves."
>
> This afternoon fifteen people can be found at any crap table at Lake Tahoe. There is no such thing as solitude here, and never again will there be.

Again, I hope this entices you to read further. The rest of the little story is just as telling. And it's contrast—between then and now—that does the telling.

Simon Wiesenthal, the Nazi hunter, says, speaking of alleged war criminals living in the United States, "When somebody smokes a marijuana cigaret, he cannot enter the United States. But when he kills a few thousand people, he can." Wham!

Kuralt is expert at finding just the right examples to prove a point. From Jackrabbit, Arizona, he reports:

I like Jackrabbit as a place, but especially as a name. Town names in Arizona have a realistic ring to them, probably because they were settled by realistic people. Oh, there are towns called Carefree and Friendly Corner and Eden in Arizona, even Inspiration and Paradise. And, of course, Phoenix. Chamber of Commerce names.

But most of those old settlers told it like it was, rough and rocky. They named their towns Rimrock, Rough Rock, Round Rock, and Wide Ruins, Skull Valley, Bitter Springs, Wolf Hole, Tombstone. It's a tough country. The names of Arizona towns tell you all you need to know.

Back east they name towns Willow Springs and Elmhurst and Appleville. Out here, where willows, elms and apples will not grow, there's a town named Greasewood and another named Cuckelbur, and another named Hackberry. That's the honest truth, you see. Yucca, Arizona. It doesn't sound as pretty as Willow Springs, but it's the truth: no willows, lots of yucca.

The example, a particular item or incident or facet that represents a group or type. Examples strengthen a generality with specificity. Martin Luther King, Jr., in his "Letter from Birmingham Jail" discussed extremism, an ism of which he was charged, explaining that it can be OK, that it can be a cause for satisfaction:

Was not Jesus an extremist in love? "Love your enemies, bless them that curse you, pray for them that despitefully use you." Was not Amos an extremist for justice—"Let justice roll down like waters and righteousness like a mighty stream." Was not Paul an extremist for the gospel of Jesus Christ—"I bear in my body the marks of the Lord Jesus." Was not Martin Luther an extremist—"Here I stand; I can do none other so help me God." Was not John Bunyan an extremist—"I will stay in jail to the end of my days before I make a butchery of my conscience." Was not Abraham Lincoln an extremist—"This nation cannot survive half slave and half free." Was not Thomas Jefferson an extremist—"We hold these truths to be self evident that all men are created equal." So the question is not whether we will be extremist but what kind of extremist will we be.

Who says exposition needs to be dull?

Identification is still another tool of exposition. Identification: the providing of context for someone or something, an orientation. Kuralt says that "Boonville (California) is not one of your automotive repair centers. There are a couple of gas stations that can give you a lube job, and five miles up the road at Philo, there's Brownie, who has a wrecker, but if you suffer a major breakdown in Boonville, you're going to be in Boonville for a while. I can assure you of that, because this is where the gallant old van that transports our CBS News crew around the country has broken down. This time." And Point Lobos, also in California, "belongs to the rocks and waves and otters and seals and birds. Man comes here as a stranger. You park well back from the coast and approach Point Lobos on foot, past a grove of fantastic gnarled and twisted Monterey cypresses, through the sea grasses and windblown chaparral. I have made this walk many times—Point Lobos is a pilgrimage—and every time I have felt small and out of place, a stranger in a perilous and majestic meeting place of land and sea."

Joseph Treaster, writing of "The Violent Streets of Luis Guzman" in the *New York Times*, tells us:

Avenue D on the Lower East Side of Manhattan is only 12 blocks long. But it is one of the meanest streets in America, a narrow corridor of poverty and violence running north from Houston Street, parallel to the East River and just across town from the leafy tranquillity of Greenwich Village.

It is a street where murders take place in the afternoon sunlight, where drug dealers operate boldly, fearing one another more than the police who occasionally cruise past in radio cars; a street where men gripping beer bottles in brown paper bags exchange prison memories, while little boys practice kung fu and karate and their mothers shop with food stamps for Cafe Bustelo and yellow rice.

It is a street of housing projects and crumbling tenements, some abandoned and burned out, a street where the language of choice is Spanish and the old men play dominoes.

For Luis Guzman, the third of six children born to an illiterate, heavy-drinking delivery truck driver and a chronically ill, listless mother, Avenue D was the center of the world.

Classification means to systematically arrange or categorize, to place in groups according to established, recognizable criteria. "They're proud of the Okefenokee," writes Charles Kuralt:

proud of its impenetrable places, proud that nobody quite knows whether there are still bears and panthers and ivory-billed woodpeckers living deep in the Okefenokee. There are places in there where nobody can go to find out.

Naturalists have Latin names for all the abundance of plants and animals that live here, I suppose, but I like the local names. Neverwets and floating hearts, spatterdocks and maiden can— those are plants. Thunderpumps—those are bitterns. Cham-chacks—those are red-headed woodpeckers. "There's a good god sitting in the hooraws," a swamp man will say. That's a pileated woodpecker in a bush.

Isaac Asimov, the very fertile science writer, says "Humanity has three classes of living nonhuman enemies.

First, there are the great predators: lions, bears, sharks, and so on. We treasure stories of Samson rending a lion and we shudder over the movie *Jaws*. Actually, however, those poor animals have been outclassed for thousands of years and could be driven to extinction with very little trouble if humanity really puts its mind to it.

Second, there are the invisible parasites: the viruses, bacteria, protozoa, worms, and so on, that, in one way or another, live at our expense and interfere with our health. These are far more dangerous than the large predators; we need only compare the Black Death (bubonic plague) of the Fourteenth Century with anything man-eating tigers could do. In the last 125 years, however, we have learned ways of dealing with the disease producers, and the danger has vastly diminished.

That leaves the third group: unwanted plants, or weeds. With very few exceptions these are not apparently dangerous in themselves and are certainly not dramatic, for they do nothing but grow. And yet in some ways they are the most insidious and dangerous of all.

A touch of class(ification) from Mr. Asimov as first published in the American Airlines magazine, *American Way*.

Which brings us back to definition, an expositional tool we've previously explored. Definition: meaning, a statement expressing the essential nature of a person, place, or thing.

So that I can finish as I began, with Kuralt, I'll quote another source first, Russell Lynes, in his essay, "Highbrow, Lowbrow, Middlebrow," which has classified our tastes ever since it was first published in *Harper's* back in 1949. "The highbrows come first," wrote Lynes.

Edgar Wallace, who was certainly not a highbrow himself, was asked by a newspaper reporter in Hollywood some years ago to define one. "What's a highbrow?" he said. "A highbrow is a man who has found something more interesting than women."

Presumably at some time in every man's life there are things he finds more interesting than women; alcohol, for example, or the World Series. Mr. Wallace has only partially defined the highbrow. Brander Matthews came closer when he said that "a highbrow is a person educated beyond his intelligence," and A.P. Herbert came closest of all when he wrote that "a highbrow is the kind of person who looks at a sausage and thinks of Picasso."

You want another definition? Kuralt gives you this from Jonesboro, Arkansas:

We are importing, I read in the paper, millions of tons of oil. How much oil is *that*? I asked myself; so I called my friend the expert.

"How many barrels in a ton?" I inquired.

"Gross ton or net ton?" he said.

"I don't know," I said.

"Well," he said, "I mean long ton or short ton?"

"I don't know," I said.

"Metric ton, avoirdupois ton, or troy ton?" he asked.

"Look," I said, "stop showing off. All I want to know is how many barrels in a ton."

"Well," he said, "maybe we'd better start at the beginning. How many gallons are in this barrel you're talking about?"

"What difference does it make?" I asked. "How many gallons are in any barrel?"

"Well," he said, "31 gallons if it's wine or beer. Thirty-one and a half if it's water, including rain water, except in four states where rain barrels are by law larger than beer barrels. If there's whiskey in the barrel, under federal law the barrel holds exactly 40 gallons. If the barrel holds fruit or vegetables, it's 105 dry quarts."

"A hundred and five dry quarts," I said.

"Yes," the expert said, "except cranberries."

"Cranberries," I said.

"Yes," he said, "a cranberry barrel is only 86 and 45/64ths dry quarts, of course."

"Of course," I said. "Well, there's oil in the barrel."

"Refined oil or crude oil?" he asked.

And on it goes, a comedy of confusion in dialogue, and yet basically all of it *defines* weights. It is exposition, an explanation. The confusion serves to enlighten.

Analysis, comparison and contrast, example, identification, classification, definition. Methods available to you for brighter and better exposition. It's hard work creating them, but your reward is a more contented reader.

Give meaning to your statistics

Don't write: "The company made $10 million in profits last year."

Write: "The company made $10 million in profits last year. That's up from $7.5 million last year, an increase of 33 per cent. And that's good."

Provide context for your statistics. Give them meaning.

And, for goodness sake (or your reader's sake), don't overuse them. The good statistic is the rare statistic.

President Reagan uses statistics well, or at least those who write his speeches do. When he spoke of the trillion dollar debt, he said that incredible figure translates into annual interest payments of more than $96 billion, which—he pointed out—is more than the combined profits of our 500 largest corporations. It is also more than the government spends on all its educational, nutritional, and medical programs. It is also a stack of thousand dollar bills 67 miles high.

He gives meaning to statistics: all that interest and all that money lost to better uses. He gives visibility to statistics: a pile of bills that high; now that's a lot of money.

Or as the writer put it in TWA's *Ambassador* magazine:

Imagine one of TWA's giant 747s flying at full cruising speed of 500 knots giving forth twin vapor trails of government forms. . .vapor trails with a total width of five feet and as long as the 747's flight on an around-the-clock basis for 38 days and nights. Such a flow of forms, 19.5 billion in number, would be equal to the forms used in the federal system in a single year.

He's not satisfied with that creative approach. He goes on:

Long forms, short forms, multi-page forms— forms with meddling questions to mystify the mind and anger the spirit, forms with small print to blearify the eyes and dull the heart, and forms with tiny spaces to crampify the hand and imprison the intellect. Forms to kill the dream.

That's the way to use statistics.

The ad goes: "If we stacked the 93 million pages of business reports issued by Dun & Bradstreet in a year, they would form a tower 27 times taller than the World Trade Center." Wow!

You can just explain the scope of a number. For instance, the cost of school violence, which has been estimated at close to $750 million, equals the salaries of 50-thousand additional teachers for the nation's school systems. It also could pay for most of the textbooks we use.

Some statistics speak eloquently or alarmingly without decoration or games. When I am advised that in San Mateo, California, 23 per cent of the boys in the ninth grade use alcohol regularly, I don't have to be played with. I'm gripped by statistics too harsh to decorate, too meaningful for games; they're more powerful played straight.

What you must decide is when to go straight and when to weave.

Your aim, with a statistic, is to make a point sink in. Well, consider how best to do it.

You've read, I'm sure, this gem:

If the earth's history could be compressed into a single year, the first eight months would be completely without life, the next two would see only the primitive creatures, mammals wouldn't appear until the second week in December, and no Homo sapiens until 11:45 p.m. on December 31. The entire period of man's written history would occupy the final 60 seconds before midnight.

Oh my, I'm late for an appointment.

Endings

And to conclude. . .

Well, obviously, the good writer wouldn't put it that way.

But every story needs an ending of some sort. A summing up. A call to arms. A twist. A quote that says it all.

An ending requires work, perhaps not so much as a beginning, but work, nevertheless. It requires planning so that what precedes leads naturally in its direction.

The reader should be left satisfied, feel that he's read something finished, something with a point clearly made, something with a unity that has moved him from start to finish almost in a circular manner.

Dick Brown did it with a quote in "Why Businessmen Can't Write" for *The Financial Post Magazine.* After much material on why and on how the problem might be alleviated, he writes:

> What's worrisome is not that good writing itself is a big problem, but that successful executives don't seem to give much of a damn about it. Listen to Richard Bevis, the English teacher at the University of British Columbia: "I try to persuade my students that a good command of English is important, and that it will help them in their careers, but I can't blame them when they don't believe me. Why should they? They look around and see all kinds of successful people who obviously can't write well."

A quote to conclude the matter, and to do it effectively. Quotes, in fact, are often used and often usable.

I recall Oscar Lewis' *The Children of Sanchez,* that riveting study of a Mexican family which is built on quotation, the words of those Lewis has studied and lived with and counseled. At the end Jesus Sanchez, the patriarch of the clan, says with both fight and resignation:

> At my age, it isn't myself I have to watch out for, but the kids. . . .
>
> I want to leave them a room, that's my ambition; to build that little house, one or two rooms or three so that each child will have a home and so they can live there together.
>
> But they don't want to help me. I asked God to

give me the strength to keep struggling so I won't go under soon and maybe finish that little house. Just a modest place that they can't be thrown out of. I'll put a fence around it and no one will bother them. It will be a protection for them when I fall down and don't get up again.

Henry Mitchell's story about Eudora Welty some years ago in the Washington *Post* ends with a quote and comment, too. She says, then he says:

> "What would really bother me was if I wrote a flop and it was praised—just out of habit. And I think things like that can happen."

Milton, of course, would have thought so, too.

A quote that summarizes is Patrick Young's way of ending "Battling the High Cost of Arthritis" in an issue of *American Way,* a quote from one of his sources:

> Max Buban summarizes: "What some of the more progressive medical directors have been able to do is to get to management and say, 'Our costs are skyrocketing and we really see as medical people that we can do some preventive medicine that will save money for the company.' But we're just in the beginning."

"The Unracked Back" is an excellent little piece in the December, 1981, *Esquire,* in which author Thomas De Carlo speaks volumes of warnings about how we misuse a part of our body that is both strong and delicate. And he reminds us again in a pithy final paragraph:

> The back is a magnificent piece of craftsmanship. With a little maintenance, a little work, it can be as wonderful to live with as it is to behold.

Sometimes you want to give a feeling of continuation as you draw an article to a close. Jimmy Breslin did in "A Hero at the Crossroads," an emotion-packed story about Vietnam. It ran in *New York* and tells of a GI, O'Malley, and the "small piece of jagged, tan-painted metal" they took out of his lung, and the Medal of Honor he won:

> "When I went to Washington and saw this major and some other people, they told me don't tell anybody about it because President Johnson

wanted to announce it himself and if it got out first, then I wouldn't get the medal. I said to myself I'll wait until I get it and then it'll mean something to me.''

He picked up the box from the bureau and took it with him. He had an affair to go to and the people had asked him to bring the medal with him so they could look at it and get excited over it and drink to its owner. He put it on the seat next to him in his small red Volkswagen and he drove away for another night that would be late.

An anecdote can wind things up, too, as Sally Quinn proved in her story on ballet legend Rudolf Nureyev in the Style section of the Washington *Post:*

He turns to the waiter and asks for a cup of tea.

"I think I am getting drunk. I want to be able to think straight. This interview is so acid it's good we didn't have vinegar with the salad.'' He laughs.

"I want to be sober when you drop the bomb question, when you do a Hiroshima on me,'' he giggles again.

Well, then, Mr. Nureyev, how's your sex life?

"I knew it, you see, there it is,'' and he clasps his hands and throws his head back and laughs with Slavic glee.

"Sporadic,'' he announces.

Well, tell us more. The ladies will be disappointed with that little morsel and nothing else.

"The ladies will just have to remain tense,'' he says sadistically.

He leans back smugly, ponders his own words, then leans forward and asks with real earnestness: "This is a city of politicians. How am I doing in this interview? Am I as good as the politicians?''

When told he has revealed absolutely nothing of himself, that he is still a complete mystery, that he is impenetrable as an interviewee, he beams like a Boy Scout receiving a medal.

"Now we must go,'' he says, his success complete. "We will pay the bill, then you will feel guilty and your conscience will make you write nice things.''

And he gets up from the table and stalks triumphantly out of the restaurant, as though he is taking bows for a magnificent performance.

As, indeed, that ending is.

Give us philosophy in an ending, as does Eugene McCarthy in an article on campaigning for *Geo*:

Defeat in politics, even relative failure, is not easy to accept. Dismissing the troops, as both Napoleon and Robert E. Lee learned, is not easy. Soldiers do not want to take their horses and mules and go back to the spring plowing.

It is better to win.

Or give us advice, as does Lewis Lapham when he stepped down recently from his position of editor at *Harper's:*

We will all need our wits about us; none of us can afford to dismiss lightly any theorem, commentary, or hypothesis arising from the wellsprings of hope, rather than the pit of fear. Among the voices of wisdom and experience, I would expect to recognize many of those to whom I have sent messages in a bottle, and from whom I received an answering note of affirmation.

Or give us humor, as does Andy Rooney in his "Sixty Minutes'' bit about ratings. He rates things one to ten, he says, and gives us a lengthy list, ending:

I rate liver one. I know I dislike liver and I don't ever want to try another piece.

The way to end a cute piece like this would be for me to give it a rating from one to ten. I rate television people who put endings like that on pieces like this, two.

But then, I'd rate Andy Rooney ten.

The story analyzed

The story is an interesting one and, potentially, fascinating: about five prominent teachers of various artistic disciplines. Elizabeth Ames wrote it for *Horizon*.

It begins with an introductory section in which the concept of "great teacher" is discussed. "A great teacher," writes Elizabeth Ames,

> can change a life: consider Anne Sullivan and her student, Helen Keller. In the arts, a great teacher can change a culture: consider Walter Gropius and his students at the Bauhaus. More than directors, impresarios, editors, critics, or gallery owners, teachers are responsible for the emergence of artistic talent—yet with few exceptions, the public doesn't even know their names.

> What makes a great teacher? In the highly competitive world of the arts, where so few become household names, it's too facile to answer, "famous students." The impact of a great teacher is both deeper and wider than the production of a star or two for the pages of *People* magazine.

> First and foremost, a great teacher is a master diagnostician. John Leggett, head of the University of Iowa's internationally known creative writing program, says an exceptional teacher is "like a doctor, able to put a finger on a student's weaknesses and strengths."

And so on. It's an appropriate beginning, paving the way as it does for a meeting, on an individual basis (in five sections), of the five selected "great teachers."

The article, in other words, is well conceived, well structured, designed so that we first get the general thrust of the piece and then the excitement of discovery as each teacher is introduced to us.

But the problem of such an article is space. *Horizon* serves an audience that qualifies as somewhat elite, as knowledgeable about the arts. So it would seem to be an audience that seeks to find out more than the rudiments of a subject tackled, since the rudiments probably already are known. In an article on "great teachers" some depth should follow the lead section. The reader should have an opportunity to gain insight, to leave the read article with more than *People*-depth knowledge. *Horizon* didn't provide enough space, and in that is a lesson for you.

Let's look at just one section of the article, the one that immediately follows the introduction. Here it is along with what I would have suggested for change as an editor committed to educating my knowing audience entertainingly:

I'd like a scene—her studio. She's working with a student—maybe E. Hynes or M. Christos, since they're quoted. Whole article could be structured around the lesson.

Ellen Faull's students—nearly eighty in all—currently include New York City Opera principals Ashley Putnam, Gianna Rolandi, Marianna Christos, and Elizabeth Hynes. Faull periodically conducts master classes around the country and is on the faculty of the Manhattan School of Music, the Mannes College of Music, and the Juilliard School. Students fly in from all over the country for her advice. Says soprano Christo: "I never like to do a role—any role—unless I work it through with her."

Imprecise, but use as a follow-up to a lead section in which you begin to show how she teaches.

A cue: How about doing just that? We'd learn a lot sitting in.

Faull's students praise her ability to correct technical problems. Christos claims Faull enabled her to develop "a whole new technique, to get my voice out front and get it bright."

Example would beef this. In narrative, the example would be almost automatically ushered in.

To see this through the author's eyes and ears would be enlightening, perhaps thrilling.

An exceptionally warm, jovial woman, Faull interrupts an explanation of her methods with

Does she laugh these words? awk.

frequent bursts of laughter: "I put people on the floor a lot. On the floor you breathe more deeply and naturally—like babies do. Everything opens up." She also makes singers wear a rib-belt girdle so they can feel the proper breathing motion in the midtorso.

Again—an example, please.

"I go by the things I feel. I'll be working with someone and a new idea will come to me." Her intuition comes from experience: Faull was once a leading soprano at the New York City Opera. From time to time, she still sings there with students, which she says can be "strange." Faull admits she must then fight the urge to listen to her proteges.

Could be elaborated. And one could make the point that some good singers (and she was no more than that) can be great teachers. (Just as some great singers probably couldn't teach at all.)

Again, it could happen in a narrative.

Singers can have tender egos: Faull handles them with kid gloves. "One of the greatest things about her is her ability to build up your confidence," says Elizabeth Hynes. Christos adds, "She never mentions anything right after a performance that she hasn't liked."

These are good. I'd like a couple more from other students. One could then have a series of potent quotes.

Both singers say Faull regularly attends their performances despite her "horrendous" schedule—and indeed she seems to form close bonds with students. Faull has made many professional referrals, and will put up singers in her home or help them financially.

Good. I'd expand some. This is an unusual aspect of the teacher-student tie, particularly, I think in the area of voice teachers. In the past, particularly, they used to be such cold and distant autocrats.

Strange to merely introduce and then drop.

Opera singers travel a difficult road and Faull "doesn't always paint a glowing picture," says Elizabeth Hynes. Still, the singer finds inspiration in Faull's example. For one thing, she says it's encouraging that her teacher "has been able to have a career like that and a normal family life. Not many singers have both."

Could we get some pointers from Faull? Would make a good windup.

The section, I'd sum up, needs expansion, enrichment. The words here merely suggest what happens in that music studio. I want my readers to be shown. Make the most of the story, not more than it deserves but the most.

And that's something for all of you to remember. When you write a story or evaluate it as editor, consider what it should do for the reader and how. Then make sure that the coverage and the writing do what you intend. Don't waste a story situation; do make the most of it.

A fictional twist

A story in *The Christian Science Monitor*, which appeared a few years ago, used a writing device available to you that's frowned upon in some quarters, particularly trade publications.

I don't know why, for fictionalization carefully used and labeled can communicate messages effectively.

The *Monitor's* Ned Temko was covering the Vienna conference of mideast oil chiefs, Saudi Arabia's Yamani and company. Here's how he began his story:

The white-robed petro-sheikhs of Saudi Arabia may be drafting an angry oilgram to President Carter that goes something like this:

HAVE HAD ENOUGH YOUR MIDEAST POLICY STOP ENOUGH CAMPAIGN PROMISES FOR ISRAEL STOP ENOUGH PALESTINIAN AUTONOMY TALKS LEADING NOWHERE STOP SEE HOW YOU LIKE THIS: WE NOW PLAN TO HIKE WORLD OIL PRICES, TRIM OIL SUPPLY.

Some experts feel such a message could turn up in the Oval Office as early as September 15 and 16, when a chaotic Organization of Petroleum Exporting Countries (OPEC) convenes a regular strategy session in Vienna.

Such a device is likely to make the reader more perceptive about the tightrope we in the United States walk trying to maintain our friendly ties with Israel and our oil supplies from friendly (and not-so-friendly) Arabs. The author makes clear that the cable is fiction, but that it expresses feelings and potentialities very much nonfiction.

If such a fictional twist occurs to you, and you're sure it helps you make a point more keenly, then why not use it?

I'm obviously not talking here about the Norman Mailer and Truman Capote efforts to rewrite fact into fiction. That's something else again, effective sure, but extremely difficult and usually out-of-place in a journalistic medium.

But when *Time* discussed a major anti-flood project in England, it did right to invoke fictionalization (to present as real something that isn't but could be):

Driven by high winds and tides, the great surge of water spills over the embankments of the Thames River and sweeps across dozens of square miles of London, endangering countless thousands of people. More than a quarter of a million homes, offices and factories in such low-lying areas as Westminster, Hammersmith, Lambeth and South-wark are inundated. In the streets, thousands of cars are left stranded. In central London, the underground is paralyzed, bridges and tunnels are closed. Hospitals struggle valiantly to maintain services, their task made all the more difficult by power blackouts, loss of telephone service, contamination of the water supply and the difficulty of mobilizing rescue teams. The Houses of Parliament and New Scotland Yard stand in several feet of water. Total damages from the great Thames flood: more than $6 billion.

This scenario is not the product of an avid Hollywood scriptwriter. It is a grim projection by British experts who know only too well that the apparently placid Thames can turn with little warning into a terrifying torment. To forestall the disaster that a "worst case" Thames flood would produce, British engineers are rushing to complete by the end of 1982 an extraordinary project: a giant, movable steel and concrete flood barrier that in normal circumstances will allow the passage of large ships but rise up during flood threats to block the menacing waters.

That paints quite a picture and thereby explains the importance of the project. Fortunately, it's fiction.

If you want to discuss new variations on the old savings account, you can do so by creating a family in which each member has a different purpose to save money and therefore benefits differently and most from one sort of account or another.

If you want to describe what might happen in a declining neighborhood should efforts to revive it not be attempted, then you can talk to the experts and with their knowledge create a stark picture of the place in a time soon to come (like Ebenezer Scrooge seeing the bleak future unless he mends his ways).

As long as: (1) you don't use the device more than rarely, (2) you enhance reality, and (3) you clearly identify the fiction as fiction—you're on safe ground.

Try it sometime.

Structural and informational devices

It's all in the packaging.

Sometimes you can impress your reader by compressing information, revealing through a heavy dosage of material within a small space how important or how fascinating or how big your subject is.

I call it clumping information.

Alvin Toffler in his book, *The Third Wave*, compresses a lot of history and makes it meaningful when he writes:

Until 1650-1750, therefore, we can speak of a First Wave World. Despite patches of primitivism and hints of the industrial future, agricultural civilization dominated the planet and seemed destined to do so forever.

This was the world in which the industrial revolution erupted, launching the Second Wave and creating a strange, powerful, feverishly energetic countercivilization. Industrialism was more than smokestacks and assembly lines. It was a rich, many-sided social system that touched every aspect of human life and attacked every feature of the First Wave past. It introduced the great Willow Run factory outside Detroit, but it also put the tractor on the farm, the typewriter in the office, the refrigerator in the kitchen. It produced the daily newspaper and the cinema, the subway and the DC-3. It gave us cubism and twelve-tone music. It gave us Bauhaus buildings and Barcelona chairs, sit-down strikes, vitamin pills, and lengthened life spans. It universalized the wristwatch and the ballot box. More important, it linked all these things together—assembled them, like a machine—to form the most powerful, cohesive and expansive social system the world had ever known: Second wave civilization.

You can do the same thing with a multi-talented and multi-active human being. You can do it with a museum or university that accomplishes many things. You can do it with a city that contributes a multitude of products and processes to our way of life. You can do it with a corporation that serves the public in very different ways.

If you really know your subject and can select the right elements to clump, then you can reveal a truth larger than its parts. But be careful. You also can distort.

What if you have a subject with various strains of information or activity? You're stumped. You don't know how to put it all together. Sometimes the answer lies in not putting it all together. The answer may be to compartmentalize.

Gigi Mahon wrote of auctions and auctioneering in our times, this for *American Way*. She realized after gathering her facts that an auction is different things. So to give us that notion, she structured the introductory section of her article into compartments:

"RAF Bombs Hamburg in 'All-Out' Attack." "Battle in Leningrad! Nazis on Outskirts." Sonja Henie applies for American citizenship, La Guardia seeks a third term, and the Brooklyn Dodgers drop an eleven-inning game to Pittsburgh.

These are headlines in newspapers dating back thirty-five years. The heirlooms they enfold are that age and older. The time is a summer afternoon, and Edie Beale sits in the conference room of a bank in East Hampton, Long Island, watching her past—and her mother's and her grandmother's—being unwrapped piece by piece before her.

The little piece goes on to explain that an auction gallery has been consigned to take these family treasures to New York to sell.

The scene switches (bullets separate item from item):

Three thousand miles away, in London, a man walks timidly into the New Bond Street offices of Sotheby's, world's oldest auction house. Carrying a large box, he approaches a high, long counter and informs one of the bright-faced young men behind it that he has some books he'd like to sell.

We find out what happens.

The scene switches again:

It is Saturday afternoon in a small town outside Chicago, a woman strolls into the local VFW hall, scene of an auction, and stops at the desk to pick up a mimeographed list of items for sale.

Sort of an auction-style rummage sale, quite different from a gallery event or a Sotheby agreement.

The scene switches once more:

In a San Francisco auction marked by otherwise uninspired bidding and prices that have not managed to break the $200 mark, the crowd is hushed and the bidding hot and heavy on a rather dilapidated wing chair. A man and woman have squared off, he a dealer, she a housewife with a vacant corner in her den. The price rises to $1,400 before the housewife drops out of the bidding. The audience bursts into spontaneous applause. It's been the best show of the day.

The successful dealer rises and moves outside, followed by six or seven other men, also dealers, from other parts of the room. They convene on the front steps and engage in a somewhat Byzantine ritual known as a "knockdown."

We find out what all that was about after the author moves on to say, "No one knows exactly where or when auctions began—perhaps when a toga-sporting young entrepreneur was struck with the realization that he possessed something that two or more people were willing to argue over."

Miss Mahon has helped herself structure a story that helps us get through it. She's compartmentalized. You can do it if, for instance, you have to write about the new corporate headquarters, giving compartments to the visitors' area with its museum of modern American paintings, to the library and research center, to the health facilities and infirmary, to the dining room and party area, to the manufacturing center, and so forth. How much easier to separate the separable than to attempt putting all together in one flowing story (which somehow won't flow no matter how hard you try).

Q and A works, too.

Not only when you actually have done an interview and wish to reproduce the results that way, as questions and answers, but also when you decide that a body of knowledge is most easily and effectively and concisely presented in that format.

The Associated Press determined to answer all of our questions about renewed draft registration. "Here, in question-and-answer form, is a discussion of the draft registration program. It is based on reports by White House press secretary Jody Powell, officials of the Selective Service System, and John White, deputy director of the Office of Management and Budget.

Q. *Who will be required to register?*

A. All men, single or married, aged 18 to 26.

Q. *Is the government about to draft young people into the armed services?*

A. The registration program does not mean a draft is imminent. But, said one official, "it is a major step" toward a draft. Actual conscription would require legislation.

Q. *When will registration begin?*

A. Within a year, and possibly as early as several months from now.

Etc. Through where and what if you don't and will there be draft cards and what about physicals. All the questions we as parents and we as potential draftees were asking were being asked for us and answered. The information is easy to learn and quick to read.

You can do it about a new benefits program or about what a new drug will do when marketed or what a new curriculum seeks to accomplish. Q and A is efficient.

Some other easy structures to create (and for readers to follow) are:

(1) Just what I'm doing now—listing by the numbers different kinds of story structures or different aspects of a revised method to get title to a car or house or the benefits you'll reap from working the bond market.

(2) Parallelism. Here's the problem and its answer. Here's the second problem and its answer. Here's the third problem and its answer. Or here's the way it used to be and this is the way it is now, once, twice, five times if necessary to cover the story.

(3) Cause and effect. This is what you do and that's what happens because of it. This is also what you do and that's what happens because of it. And the third thing you do is such-and-such and when you do that, this happens.

(4) Chronology. Tell your story as it happens in real life—here's how to build your patio, step by step, chronologically; or here's what happened on the day the Smasgurgians invaded Cosmotania, chronologically; or here are the highlights from my vacation in Antarctica in diary form, chronologically.

Think of the information you have and how best to put it all together. Information should guide organization, not the opposite. Don't impose structure. Let it emerge from what the material suggests. Works better that way.

The use of quotes

Recently I had an opportunity to participate in the Penton/IPC Conference on Editorial Creativity in Cleveland. My pleasure was to talk about writing to 150 or more editors. My entertainment was listening to other speakers, among them T. George Harris, former editor of *Psychology Today* and now contributing editor of *Industry Week*.

Mr. Harris keynoted the affair, addressing the topic, "The Editor Shapes the Character of the Magazine." Well, he not only provided information, but he prompted this column, the use of quotes. You see, I took pages of notes based on what he said. Most of the time I paraphrased, since I do not use shorthand. But occasionally *how* he said *what* he said was so effective, I struggled to set down the words as he spoke them.

Informally I was going through the same selection process that any writer must who deals with a speech or interview or series of interviews. Looking through the notes, I perked when I spotted those direct quotes.

Let me share a few with you. They're educational as information and viewpoint, not merely good examples of what I'm discussing with you in this particular column.

"Editing is having a sense of what you're after, not just or primarily dealing with language precision," he said.

"As editor give yourself totally to the logic of the idea rather than the rules," he said.

"The editor is a creator of a community," he said.

"An editor should free up his staff to work beyond their capacities," he said.

"Editorial creativity comes down to a person the reader knows," he said.

"The role of the editor is an act of passionate listening," he said.

I reacted to these comments when Mr. Harris spoke them. I reacted to them again when scanning the notes. I would not have reacted quite so strongly the second time if I had immersed them in lots and longer quotes. And that, of course, is where writers sometimes go wrong. They either get too fond of too many statements a speaker speaks, or they are too lazy to figure out which of the quotes are telling

enough to be used verbatim rather than in altered form.

A writer can make or break the power of a quote, depending on where he places it and in what context he places it. Here's a page from a speech given by a friend of mine, A. Sherburne Hart, vice president of public affairs for Union Carbide. Hart spoke these words along with numerous others to Michigan's Chemical and Allied Trade Council in January:

> It is time we began to point out, loudly and unequivocally, that the performance, policies, and commitments of the chemical industry are so demanding that they are already protecting the public from the health risks of chemicals. The burden of accusations against us consists almost invariably of the same three or four public incidents, repeated over and over again.
>
> When accusations against us are simply wrong or vague or twenty years old, we have to say so, and use the media to make sure everybody gets the message. The EPA made the public charge that there may be as many as 50,000 potentially hazardous waste disposal sites in this country, and pumped it through the media to a point where it has become common wisdom. The fact is that nobody has yet come up with more than some 500 potentially hazardous sites. That's an error factor of 100 times, and it was flaunted with impunity because the EPA knew we wouldn't take them on. It's time that we committed ourselves to seeing to it that when anybody makes a serious charge against the industry, they had better have their facts straight first.
>
> It is also time we made clear that when any health problems associated with chemicals are even suspected, that we act immediately and responsibly to deal with them, no matter what the cost; and that we do not excuse or condone or commiserate with the failures of any company or employee in our industry who does not meet these high standards.
>
> If we can reach the public on these issues—the ones that matter most—they will begin to listen to us on other matters. They'll acknowledge the critical role of the chemical industry in our economy, in providing jobs and exports, and they'll give a fair hearing to our demands for government policies that enable us to compete

successfully in world markets. They'll acknowledge our awesome contributions to the development of new technologies and our need for resources to invest in research and development.

The whole segment is quotable because a point important to Hart and his company is being made, and he makes the point succinctly enough. But as a reporter and writer I'd have to make choices:

> Hart called on the chemical industry to speak out "loudly and unequivocally" when critics attack the industry's commitment to safety. He spoke of policies and performance of such rigor that the public should feel secure.

> "The burden of accusations against us," he said, "consists almost invariably of the same three or four public incidents, repeated over and over again."

> Hart noted a charge from the Environmental Protection Agency that there may be 50,000 potentially hazardous waste disposal sites in this country. Not so, he said. There are 500, "an error factor of 100 times." When that happens, Hart added, the industry should not remain silent. "It's time that we committed ourselves to seeing. . .that when anybody makes a serious charge against the industry, they had better have their facts straight first."

> Hart placed responsibility on his own industry, too, insisting that when any health problems associated with chemicals arise, there should be immediate action. He stressed also that everyone in the industry must meet high standards, that failures should not be excused or condoned.

> If all that happens, he said, the public may begin to listen. Perhaps then, he concluded, the public will "acknowledge the critical role of the chemical industry in our economy, in providing jobs and exports."

And so forth. The mix of direct and indirect quotes makes a more readable speech story.

The mix of quotes and no quotes makes a better story.

The strong quote stands out when what surrounds it looks different, when context and buildup encircle it.

I recall Pranay Gupte's report from Baghdad in the *New York Times* a while back, a report about the Iraq-Iran war as seen from a people's point of view far from the battlelines. We are introduced to a family:

> The house that Achmat Hassan built five years ago with an interest-free government loan is set behind a small courtyard whose walls shield it from the traffic noise of Aziz street. A tiny date palm rises in the courtyard, and around it play Mr. Hassan's three children, who range downward in age from 4 years old. They do not fully understand that their father will not be coming home anymore.
>
> "We are told he died a martyr," said Mr. Hassan's teen-age sister, Nouaal. "Martyr for what? How many more martyrs before we can have peace again?"
>
> Achmat Hassan was a soldier in the Iraqi army; he was killed a few days ago. . . .

A powerful quote because of its passion and because of its positioning. As in this lead section from William Borders' Italian earthquake report in the same newspaper:

> SANT'ANGELO DE'LOMBARDI, Italy—At a crossroads not far from this little mountain town, a road worker in a red wool coat stopped shoveling for a moment this afternoon to reply to a stranger's question about directions.
>
> "Sant'Angelo is 14 kilometers that way, sir," he said, gesturing with his cloth cap toward the next hilltop. "But there isn't anything left of it."

Quotes can help make good leads, although writers and editors should be careful to save quotes for those leads in which they really can make an impact. The quote lead should not be overused.

> "I don't want to be anymore the one that sings the most, but the one that sings the *best*," emphasizes Placido Domingo in his charmingly accented, fluent English. The handsome Madrid-born opera star, who is considered by many. . .to be the world's greatest tenor, better even than his more famous rival, Luciano Pavarotti, nods several times, as if to convince himself of his determination to shatter his Superman of Song image.

That's how the story on the tenor by Naomi Graffman begins in the Amtrak magazine. A good quote, so why not feature it?

When Daniel Lehman approached the subject "Abuse Begins at Home"—a look at adult homes—in *The Village Voice,* he started with a quote:

"All I wanted was a decent breakfast instead of that rot they had been serving us," Barbara Brubaker tells me. "But the administrator of that adult home looked at me and told me something I'll never forget. 'You know,' he told me, 'if you were in a concentration camp and complained like that, you would be shot.' "

And then there's the story about Oakland I came across:

The story is told that Gertrude Stein, who spent her girlhood in Oakland, once said that the problem with Oakland was, "When you get there, there isn't any THERE there."

We're assured by the writer that the assessment is more clever than it is true.

Use the quote sparingly, carefully, emphatically. That way it'll gain the reader's attention, as is your purpose.

Tidbits

"I think the following rules will cover most cases," writes George Orwell in his eassy, "Politics and the English Language":

(i) Never use a metaphor, simile or other figure of speech which you are used to seeing in print.

(ii) Never use a long word where a short one will do.

(iii) If it is possible to cut a word out, always cut it out.

(iv) Never use the passive where you can use the active.

(v) Never use a foreign phrase, a scientific word or a jargon word if you can think of an everyday English equivalent.

(vi) Break any of these rules sooner than say anything outright barbarous.

The element of paradox gains you attention. So when someone people expect to say or do one thing says or does another, when conditions result in the opposite of the predicted, when an argument originates from the contradictory or blossoms strangely, when assumptions or deductions counter the anticipated, then by all means make the most of the opportunity.

"We can never forget," wrote Martin Luther King, Jr., "that everything Hitler did in Germany was 'legal' and everything the Hungarian freedom fighters did in Hungary was 'illegal.' It was 'illegal' to aid and comfort a Jew in Hitler's Germany. But I am sure that, if I had lived in Germany during that time, I would have aided and comforted my Jewish brothers even though it was illegal. If I lived in a communist country today where certain principles dear to the Christian faith are suppressed, I believe I would openly advocate disobeying these antireligious laws."

Avoid using such words as *think* and *believe* as in "The President thinks. . ." and "The professor believes. . ."

You don't really know what the President thinks or the professor believes. All you really know is what he or she says he or she believes, or what others say he or she believes. Therefore, it's more accurate (and safer) to write that "The President voiced the thought that. . ." and "The professor expressed a belief in. . ." Or even, "The professor said she believes. . ."

"Feels" poses a similar problem.

Granted, the hedge can make your words more awkward. But diplomacy or fear or self-aggrandizement can make a person emit words distant from the actual emotional mullings in the brain.

If you want your narrative to gain immediacy, then see if using present tense verbs does the job for you. They can give the reader a feeling of sharing an event as it is happening, and that can conjure visions quite powerful.

If you want your interview story or roundup to gain immediacy, then see if using present tense versions of "say" does the job for you. Opinions expressed last week or last month would most likely be expressed the same way now or a month from now. So you needn't make the comment past tense. Let it be said at the moment of reading; the information may gain in timeliness and timelessness.

Was it Chekhov who warned playwrights not to hang a gun over the fireplace in act one unless it's meant to go off before the final curtain? Well, whoever. It makes sense for all writers.

For a good story you're supposed to have gathered more information than you can use. So don't use everything you've gathered. Make sure you use only that which furthers the theme and flow of your story.

Be highly self-critical. Be highly selective. Put in just what needs to go in. Keep the rest out.

Flow. Can it be over-emphasized? No. Sentence must merge into sentence, paragraph into paragraph, idea into idea. Your reader should know at once where he is, where he's been, and where he is likely to go. And why, I might add.

And don't you know there is no captive audience?

So you won't pitch the pitch

We can learn about writing from those who want our support. The search for charitable funds makes language flower.

And why not? Good causes deserve good words as good words deserve good causes.

Father Bruce Ritter, the founder of Covenant House, is one of the best. He plays, quite rightly, on our compassion. "Please, read what I have to tell you," he begins, the "Please" underlined in blue. "Children," he goes on,

> . . .are being sold. Their bodies and spirits are being corrupted. They are forced into a life of abuse and degradation.
>
> Where?
>
> India? Uganda? Peru?
>
> No!
>
> Right here in New York, the Big Apple, Fun City.
>
> Covenant House began as a response to the needs of these children of the streets. Will you join with me in helping to carry out this work?

He has posed the problem, and note how compellingly. Now he must support his plea with background and with the scope of the dilemma:

> One night in the winter of 1969, six teenage runaways knocked on the door of the tenement apartment where I was living to serve the poor on New York's Lower East Side. I took them in. The next day, four more came. I could not turn them away. And they have been coming ever since. That, in essence, is how Covenant House was born.
>
> Today, most of the efforts of Covenant House are concentrated on the sordid streets of the infamous Minnesota Strip, a fifteen block stretch of Eighth Avenue from New York's Port Authority bus terminal to the lower Fifties. This is an area filled with porno parlors, strip joints, cheap bars, fleabag hotels and thousands of drifters, hookers and pimps.
>
> It is no place for a child!
>
> Yet it acts as a magnet for thousands of the estimated one million children who run away from home each year in our country.
>
> Whose children are these? Whose sons? Whose daughters? Nieces? Nephews? They are ours! Yours and mine!

Note how Father Ritter brings the problem closer to us: "Whose children are these? . . . Yours and mine!" Language to strike a responsive chord.

But the situation needs to be focused, to be personified, exemplified. The good Father does that, too:

> Take Veronica, for example. She was only eleven years old when I met her. She had already been arrested eight times for prostitution on Eighth Avenue. The authorities never bothered to check her age so that she could be referred to Family Court and receive care. Each time she was taken to the adult criminal court. Each time the judge would fine her $100. And each time her pimp, sitting in the back row, paid for it and put her back on the street.
>
> Veronica was killed shortly after she celebrated her twelfth birthday. She was thrown out of a tenth-story window, either by her pimp or a customer.
>
> There was a time when I had to turn kids away because there simply was no room. I don't do that anymore. I know only too well what happens to them.

Emotion-packed writing, to be sure, but certainly in keeping with the subject matter. Passionate so we will be compassionate.

The tone is quite different in Arthur M. Wood's letter. Mr. Wood is chairman of the Art Institute of Chicago. Before he asks me for another contribution, in the last short paragraph of a long letter, he entices me to the museum with news of the new:

> There is always an excellent reason for visiting the Art Institute—and there isn't a day when a stroll through the museum won't reveal something of very special interest. But right now it is my great pleasure to give you an even better reason to visit: to view a just-acquired painting of the rarest quality—*Vuillard's Landscape: Window Overlooking the Hills.* One of the most monumental landscapes ever painted in France in the 19th century, this glorious picture came to us through the generosity of an anonymous donor and contributions from the Major Acquisitions Fund. It was created at the end of the most productive and important decade in Vuillard's career and adds to

the strength of our fine collection of Vuillard's works. This complex, subtle work, deserving your quiet, attentive reflection, may be seen in Gallery 201.

He appeals to my intellect, what there is of it, with his more measured words, and to my obvious enthusiasm for art, since I am a contributing member to the Art Institute.

The environmentalists tend to arouse fear to make their pitch, to reach my pocket or checkbook, which sometimes I make available to them. The Sierra Club reminds me of the work it's been doing in my behalf, raising fear all the way:

> Just a short while ago, one million Americans signed a petition circulated by the Sierra Club, calling for the removal from office of James Watt, the reckless, environment-threatening Secretary of Interior.

> While other organizations also spoke out against Secretary Watt, it was the Sierra Club that mounted this unprecedented citizen's action campaign so that the President and each and every member of Congress was made fully aware of the magnitude of public protest against Mr. Watt's dangerous policies.

> But delivering those million names to Congress was not the end of our battle. Only the beginning.

> At this very moment, the Sierra Club is at work around the clock to support our dramatic petition drives with intensive political action, backed in turn by the grassroots support of our 275,000 members. And, we hope, backed by you and your membership.

> Unless you and I act immediately, we will surely witness the destroying of lands needed for our national parks, the despoiling of pristine wilderness areas, and the irreparable damage to the life-giving habitat for our nation's wildlife.

Act out of fear, that letter tells me, or at least concern. So does one from the Union of Concerned Scientists, an outfit that never minces words. Right out with it:

> "We are in a race against time."

> That's what Bob Pollard, a nuclear safety engineer for the Union of Concerned Scientists, said in January, 1979.

Bob and other UCS scientists were calling for the shutdown of the nuclear power plant at Three Mile Island—a warning that was tragically ignored. Two months later, the terrifying accident occurred.

> Today we are still in a race against time.

> USC studies have pinpointed an alarming number of acute—and still uncorrected—safety problems in dozens of nuclear power plants now operating around the country.

A quote to catch us. The problem as perceived by this organization. Then come the examples in a list: Indian Point, Zion, Diablo Canyon, these to drive home the point. "We must have your support. . .," I'm warned, lest there be no tomorrow.

The Environmental Defense Fund, meanwhile, warns me:

> The protection of endangered species may be eliminated—if big mining, timber, oil, and other commercial interests have their way!

> If that happens, the real losers will be the bald eagle, California sea otter, hawksbill sea turtle, whooping crane, and hundreds of other species already balanced precariously on the brink of extinction.

> Time is running out for the Endangered Species Act—and for the animals and plants it protects.

I'm reminded to send in my renewal.

I'm given something special if I respond to violinist Isaac Stern and his Friends of Carnegie Hall:

> Several times each year, a most unusual event takes place at Carnegie Hall.

> No tickets are sold, the Hall is two-thirds empty, admission is by invitation only. And what takes place is, for a music lover, an enthralling experience.

> This is a Dress Rehearsal, with some of the world's most celebrated musicians, as they shape, refine and perfect their work. It is an opportunity to witness the birth of a concert performance—the thoughts, feelings and craftsmanship that bring music to life. . . .

I would like to invite you to share the Dress

Rehearsal experience as a Friend of Carnegie Hall. It is just one of the privileges you will enjoy as a Friend.

Please notice there's always a gimmick to these appeals, and I don't use the word with offensiveness in mind. These people are trying to sell me. They've considered approach carefully. What words will reach me? What message? What motive?

You might consider that when you're writing a story. What sort of words will reach your reader? What message are you passing along? What motives are you trying to give birth to or awaken?

The food shortage in Poland "is desperate," Care's Alertgram tells me. Alertgram. That alone gives me pause in the day's occupation. "Thousands are going hungry as food supplies dwindle." No waste of words. Get right to it. The problem is acute, so act. Now. Perhaps by telegram to answer the Alertgram. The technique might work for you when you're trying to get your readers to write their members of Congress or state legislators. Top the page with something such as Alertgram or Telewatch or Actionwire, then state vividly and succinctly what you want done.

Help is the request in all these letters. But the words always are different. Writers have been at work considering what sort of appeal will work. Fund-raisers do what you should do. Consider what will appeal to your readership.

Recent federal budget cuts have seriously reduced student aid funds available to Northwestern students. These cuts, which total $1.7 million for the. . .academic year, affect not only grant programs but also reduce educational loan and work programs.

So help make up the difference. Give.

After nearly half a century of abuse and neglect, Central Park—one of the finest examples of landscape art in the world—is beginning to make a comeback. Grassy meadows that have been trampled bare by millions of feet are being reseeded; the weedy undergrown that choked once beautiful vistas is being cleared. . .

So help us do the job. Give.

Stories of success travel fast. And by now, you have most likely heard that the past year was a spectacular one for Lyric Opera of Chicago. All the elements—artistic, financial, administrative— fell into place for one of Lyric's best years ever. But we can't stop now.

So keep us rolling along. Give.

". . .when he drinks, he curses and smashes things, and sometimes he beats on me and the kids."

During her first night at The Salvation Army Emergency Lodge, Ann told me her story. She spoke slowly and painfully. She cried a few times.

So understand her plight. That tragic experience is echoed by so many others. Help us help them. Give.

"Starvation? No, malnutrition!" The words follow two pictures, on the left a heart-rending photo of an emaciated "Edna Maria, June 5, without HOPE," on the right a somewhat better fed "Edna Maria, June 12, after a week of HOPE." There are thousands upon thousands of other Edna Marias, we're reminded, after that photographic display. Give.

By now I'm sure you get the drift of my message. You can learn from those who raise money. They write to communicate a message they deem important. So should you. You should write to communicate *your* important message, *really* communicate it, even if it is merely the announcement of this year's national conference or a rundown of the autumn lecture series.

I can't resist the power of one more excerpt. The letterhead name is Glenn Ford, just that. And before he even says, "Dear Friend," he (or his very sharp writers) shares these words:

- The Nazis did not systematically exterminate six million Jews and millions of non-Jews.

- The ovens in Nazi concentration camps were used only to bake bread, not to cremate people.

- The poison gas in the camps was used only to kill lice, not people.

- The thousands of books about the holocaust are based on falsified information and photos.

- Anne Frank's diary was a fraud.

- Testimonies at the historic Nuremberg war-crimes trials were coerced and untrue.

- Adolf Eichmann's trial was a frame-up by the Jewish people.

- The holocaust is a hoax perpetrated on the world by Jewish propagandists.

Horrendous statements. My mind and heart are caught up in such perverse hogwash, which is exactly what Ford and friends meant to do. After the "Dear Friend," he writes:

As one of the first Americans to enter Dachau after World War II, I can personally attest to the fact that the above statements are blatant lies. The scenes of horror I witnessed at that concentration camp will haunt me forever. So when I hear such preposterous claims whitewashing Nazi brutality, I am enraged. And I find it frightening to believe that anyone could believe these outrageous lies. But the fact remains that these lies are beginning to be believed.

The seeds of doubt about the existence of the Holocaust have been planted and are already taking root in the minds of many. . . .

I'm led to immediate renewal of my membership in the Simon Wiesenthal Center.

That's writing for action.

And there's a lesson in it for you. Study "pitch" material that comes to you. At the most, you may want to contribute. At the least, you'll find words in action and techniques that may help you write more forcefully.

Bits of advice

Three bits of advice.

One: Make your first words count.

Two: Lead with your strongest element.

Three: Make your story complete.

I see frequently the results of not following these little rules.

When, for instance, one reads a story which begins, ''A seminar to discuss occupational health hazards and point out what industry is doing to eliminate them was sponsored recently by Company X at its A-B-C Laboratory for Toxicology and Industrial Medicine,'' then one sees the work of a writer not devoted to the first bit of advice. He or she is not making the first words count.

Better would be to say, ''Elimination of occupational health hazards was the concern of speakers addressing. . . .'' Or much better would be to take a quote that was buried six or more paragraphs down, the words of a speaker: ''Death is an irreversible toxicity, and we should do everything to try to avoid it.'' Now that would make a much more fetching start. Make those first words count.

Or when a writer tells me, ''On July 5, running through to the end of the month, H-I-J Gallery will present an exciting exhibition of photographs by. . .,'' then again I know that those first words are being wasted. Better to be told, ''Architectural contrasts in urban landscapes are featured in the photographs of. . . .'' Or even better yet, we might give the reader two or three brief descriptions of samples from the show to get the story underway.

Surely the writers above did not consider use of the strongest element. Holding a seminar is not as strong an element as something that was said or accomplished. When and where an exhibition is being held does little to capture the reader; what the exhibition will have in it does more.

And for the same reasons don't lead an appointment or promotion story this way: ''John Johnson Smith, chairman of the Anti-Seaweed Society of North America, announced today the hiring of Jane Janice Brown as new president of the society.'' Who makes the announcement usually is of less importance and less interest than what the announcement is. ''The founder of the Annual Insect Marathon and longtime head of the International Free the Fish from Fish Tanks Association has been named president of. . .'' is the way the story should have started.

Then, you see, you can quote John Johnson Smith on the reason why Jane Janice Brown was selected. And you can quote Jane Janice Brown on what she plans to do now that she has this new and most significant post. All that would follow the third bit of advice, which is to make the story complete.

The appointment story is not complete unless and until we get who was named and why and what's going to happen now that the naming has occurred. We should also find out, as readers, what the Anti-Seaweed Society of North America does, has done, and will continue to do.

The health hazards meeting story is not complete until we find out what matters were considered, what important things were said, and what's likely to result from the meeting.

The photography exhibit story is not complete until we find out more about the pictures and the picture taker, until we hear from the picture taker and perhaps some critics.

But the picture taker story might be even better, even more complete, if the writer went to talk to the photographer and watched the photographer at work. The health hazards item might be even better, even more complete, if the writer went to the laboratories of some who attended the session to find out what sort of research is underway in this field, and if the writer then went to various places of business where those new anti-hazard techniques are being used. The appointment story might be even better, even more complete, if the writer undertook an exploration of the Anti-Seaweed Society of North America and permitted us to see what this fascinating outfit does, and/or if the writer did a profile of Jane Janice Brown and how she runs the Annual Insect Marathon and what she's managed to accomplish with the International Free the Fish from Fish Tanks Association.

Which really leads me to a fourth bit of advice: Make the most of your story.

To do all this, you merely need to think before you write.

Ads teach

Ads sell. At least that's what they're meant to do: sell products.

But they can sell ideas, concepts, philosophies, too. And they can give advice.

For you, the writer and editor, here are some recent cullings and gleanings to give you guidance, to give you thought, to give you pause, to give you inspiration.

Chemical Bank says: "Tradition is something to build on, not to rest on." Your publication benefits when and if you remember that.

A rival bank, Manufacturer's Hanover, tells us: "The marketplace demands sustained effort." To keep your publication on people's minds and in people's hands, you have to keep trying, and trying harder.

And keeping in mind that marketplace, consider the words from United Telecom: "Our future: being purposefully distinctive." Aha. You better be. Your writing. Your design. Your journalistic approach. Be purposefully distinctive, and thereby beat your competition. Incidentally, that competition may be another publication. It may be television and lounging in the sun. It may be sleep.

The former president of the American Business Press, Charlie Mill, was quoted in an ABP ad: "The real glory of an editor lies in the editorial excellence of his publication." You editors need to remind yourselves of that. And while you're at it, remind your publishers.

An advertisement for a new magazine called *Zoom* (subtitled the *International Image Magazine*) tells us that it's all about photography and about photographic portfolios of excellence, but what caught my eye was the statement: "Every issue is a lasting record of contemporary life, *never* to be thrown away." Never to be thrown away. "Never" is a dubious absolute, of course, but you should be writing and editing and compiling a publication that its readers find very difficult to toss. You want to create a publication that is worth storing and worth using again and again.

One way you make that possible is by knowing your audience, its wants and needs and aspirations. *Cosmopolitan* keeps reminding me of that important editorial responsibility. That gorgeous lady looks at me from the full page newspaper ad. "Deliver me from the dynasty-builder," she says, "the man who looks at you as the possible mother of his future little heirs first, you as a person second. And if you marry such a man, he always cares more about them than about you. With so many adorable men out there, why bother with one of the spooks! My favorite magazine agrees. It was actually they who convinced me I'm pretty special on my own, that I don't have to get my identity from a man or children though I love both. I also love that magazine. I guess you could say I'm That COSMOPOLITAN Girl." Talk about dreams and aspirations, from the looks to the message! Do you understand your readers' dreams and aspirations? You should.

That takes me very smoothly to an ad run periodically by *Good Housekeeping,* a beautiful message about magazines and reading, which includes the following two paragraphs:

The act of reading is essentially a process of thinking. It has scan and scope beyond any camera—as you have just demonstrated on the cosmic screen of your own mind. It is a concentratively individual act. An involvement. The reader makes the printed communication happen . . .releases the magic that causes words on a page to leap into living thoughts, ideas, emotions.

And no matter how many millions may be on the receiving end of the message, it is addressed to, and received by *individuals,* one at a time—each in the splendid solitude of his or her own mind. There, the silent language of print can whisper, rage, implore, accuse, burst into song, explode into revelation, stab the conscience. Or work a healing faith. And so it will always be, come hell, high water or McLuhan.

Do you consider your public in terms of individuals rather than a mass? Do you address your articles, your information toward a person (singular) rather than persons (plural)? I'd recommend it.

A Magazine Publishers Association ad, part of a new series that keeps reminding us, "Nothing opens your eyes like a magazine," contains the statement: ". . .someone has to keep reminding them [writers] that they have something important on their minds and that there's a world out there waiting for them to put it on paper." Well, keep reminding your writers. Keep reminding yourself.

There's much information in a whole series of ads from International Paper Company about communicating better. The one that inspired me was written by poet James Dickey. "How to enjoy poetry," he says: "From the beginning, men have known that words and things, words and actions, words and feelings, go together, and that they can go together in thousands of different ways, according to who is using them. Some ways go shallow, and some go deep." Think on these things. And also he says, when you really feel poetry, "a new part of you happens, or an old part is renewed, with surprise and delight at being what it is." Poetry does that best, I agree. But good prose can do it, too. And later he says:

What is more fascinating than a rock, if you really feel it and *look* at it, or more interesting than a leaf?

Horses, I mean; butterflies, whales;
Mosses, and stars; and gravelly
Rivers, and fruit.

Oceans, I mean; black valleys; corn;
Brambles, and cliffs; rock, dirt, dust, ice. . .

Go back and read this list—it is quite a list, Mark Van Doren's list!—item by item. Slowly: Let each of these things call up an image out of your own life.

Think and feel. What moss do you see? Which horse? What field of corn? What brambles are *your* brambles? Which river is most yours?

Do you think about words and what they mean?

And do you listen? "Listening can improve your vision," says an ad from Sperry. "Good listeners think more broadly—because they hear and understand more facts and points of view. They make better innovators. . . .Ultimately, good listeners attune themselves more closely to where the world is going. . ." You'll be a better journalist if you listen.

Practical advice comes to you, too, along with the visionary nudges. In another of those International Paper ads, this one by *Reader's Digest* editor-in-chief Edward T. Thompson, we are told "How to write clearly." You really should get hold of the full text (down at the bottom we're told that reprints are available from International Paper Co., Dept. 4-B, P.O. Box 900, Elmsford, NY 10523). But to give you an idea of what Thompson offers, I mention some of the basics he includes: outline what you want to say; start where your readers are; avoid jargon; use familiar combinations of words; stick to the point, and be as brief as possible.

One more example. From Rodale Press and its extremely well-written ads on science and environment and a better future, there's this lead in the sixth of the series, an ad titled "The Losing of America": "The United States will lose 26 square miles of its land today. It will lose another 26 square miles tomorrow, and every day this year. But not to a foreign power. We are giving up our land to the ravenous demands of an unrealistic food system." And so on. Startling use of statistics, to gain our attention.

These ads have caught my attention. They had something to say. They taught.

Advice from experts

When it comes to writing, some experts really are experts. They know what they're talking about.

From William Zinsser (*On Writing Well*, Harper and Row):

Who is this elusive creature, the reader? He is a person with an attention span of about twenty seconds. He is assailed on every side by forces competing for his time: by newspaper and magazines, by television and radio and stereo, by his wife and children and pets, by his house and his yard and all the gadgets that he has bought to keep them spruce, and by that most potent of competitors, sleep. The man snoozing in his chair with an unfinished magazine open on his lap is a man who was being given too much unnecessary trouble by the writer.

It won't do to say that the snoozing reader is too dumb or too lazy to keep pace with the train of thought. My sympathies are with him. If a reader is lost, it is generally because the writer has not been careful enough to keep him on the path.

This carelessness can take any number of forms. Perhaps a sentence is so excessively cluttered that the reader, hacking his way through the verbiage, simply doesn't know what it means. Perhaps a sentence has been so shoddily constructed that the reader could read it in any of several ways. Perhaps the writer has switched pronouns in mid-sentence, or has switched tenses, so the reader loses track of who is talking or when the action took place. Perhaps Sentence B is not a logical sequel to Sentence A—the writer, in whose head the connection is clear, has not bothered to provide the missing link. Perhaps the writer has used an important word incorrectly by not taking the trouble to look it up.

So, it's up to you. It is your care and your logic and your precision and your enthusiasm that determine whether the reader (at least the loyal one) stays with you.

From Jacques Barzun (*Simple and Direct, A Rhetoric for Writers*, Harper and Row):

. . .the price of learning to use words is the development of an acute self-consciousness. Nor is it enough to pay attention to words only when you face the task of writing—that is like playing the violin only on the night of the concert. You must attend to words when you read, when you speak, when others speak. Words must become ever present in your waking life, an incessant concern, like color and design if the graphic arts matter to you, or pitch and rhythm if it is music, or speed and form if it is athletics. Words, in short, must be *there*, not unseen and unheard, as they probably are and have been up to now.

It is proper for the ordinary reader to absorb the meaning of a story or description as if the words were a transparent sheet of glass. But he can do so only because the writer has taken pains to choose and adjust them with care. They were not glass to him, but mere lumps of potential meaning. He had to weigh them and fuse them before his purposed meaning could shine through.

So, do you struggle with words, think carefully about them, combine them so they mean what you really want them to mean, wrestle them into shape, master and nurture them?

From E.B. White (*The Elements of Style*, with William Strunk, Macmillan):

"Omit needless words!" cries the author on page 21, and into that imperative Will Strunk really put his heart and soul. . . .

He was a memorable man, friendly and funny. Under the remembered sting of his kindly lash, I have been trying to omit needless words since 1919, and although there are still many words that cry for omission and the huge task will never be accomplished, it is exciting to me to reread the masterly Strunkian elaboration of this noble theme. It goes: "Vigorous writing is concise. A sentence should contain no unnecessary words, a paragraph no unnecessary sentences, for the same reason that a drawing should have no unnecessary lines and a machine no unnecessary parts. This requires not that the writer make all his sentences short, or that he avoid all detail and treat his subjects only in outline, but that every word tell."

There you have a short, valuable essay on the nature and beauty of brevity—sixty-three words that could change the world.

So, as you can surmise, Strunk was White's teacher. White brought Strunk's volume of wisdom up to date and added his introduction. Are you omitting needless words?

From Strunk himself (same book, same publisher):

Before beginning to compose something, gauge the nature and extent of the enterprise and work from a suitable design. Design informs even the simplest structure, whether of brick and steel or of prose. You raise a pup tent from one sort of vision, a cathedral from another. This does not mean that you must sit with a blueprint always in front of you, merely that you had best anticipate what you are getting into. To compose a laundry list, a writer can work directly from the pile of soiled garments, ticking them off one by one. But to write a biography the writer will need at least a rough scheme; he cannot plunge in blindly and start ticking off fact after fact about his man, lest he miss the forest for the trees and there be no end to his labors.

So, organize your material before you write. It makes the writing easier. A plan also makes changes in plan easier. Believe Strunk.

From Jerome Kelley (*Magazine Writing Today*, Writer's Digest Books):

Let's take a look at the verb "walk," which means to move unhurriedly on foot. Even at best, this is an unexciting word. But let's consider some verbs that are almost synonymous. If the person doing the walking "rambled," his journey was probably a rather aimless one. If he "hiked," he was probably in the country. If he "marched," he was going somewhere with the military. "Parading" might mean he was walking up Fifth Avenue on Easter Sunday. If he "sauntered," he could well be an individual of dubious character. "Strolling" could mean he was with the love of his life. If he was "traipsing," he might be walking idly. "Mushing" would put him behind a dog sled tracking across the frozen Arctic wastes. If he was "moseying" about, he could be a western sheriff ferreting out clues, while "promenading" could put the same sheriff in the middle of a square dance.

Each of the above words has its own shading that can impart a different meaning when used in place of "walk" in a sentence. Never choose a verb that is only serviceable; choose one that will work hard to push your sentence and the reader forward. Always use active verbs and avoid those of the passive or neutral variety. Passive verbs and passive constructions are a certain kiss of death.

"Percival kissed her" is short, strong and direct. "She was kissed by Percival" is limp.

So, consider your words of action carefully. Good writers do.

From William Rivers (*Writing: Craft and Art*, Prentice-Hall):

Writing sequentially requires another complex operation: anticipating how readers' thoughts will move. The following passage shows how easy it is to forget readers:

" 'Astrology, palmistry, phrenology, life reading, fortune telling, cartomancy, clairvoyance, clairaudience, crystal gazing, hypnotism, mediumship, prophecy, augury, divination, magic or necromancy' for money are illegal activities in Palo Alto and licensed businesses in Menlo Park. Both laws have been on the books for forty years and read as though they came from a Model Government Game, with blanks to fill in, permitted or not permitted."

"Both laws"? When the reader comes upon those words, his mind says that no law has been mentioned. The long series of unusual words in the first sentence makes him concentrate on them (while puzzling over a quotation attributed to no one); he cannot think of "illegal activities" and "licensed businesses" in terms of law. He probably would not have thought of them as laws anyway. An activity is illegal as a result of a law, a business is licensed because of a law; neither is a law. Moreover, the analogy of the "Modern Government Game" in the second sentence makes the reader use his imagination, which he can't do while puzzling over "Both laws." To understand "Both laws," the reader must look back at the first sentence to trace the meaning, which halts his reading and irritates him.

This error can be corrected by treating "illegal activities" and "licensed businesses" in terms of laws in the first sentence: ". . .illegal in Palo Alto and permitted by law in Menlo Park." The ease of correcting may make the principle seem unimportant, but if we do not think sequentially in small matters, we may be powerless with larger ones.

The largest problem in writing coherently grows out of the infinite number of ways we can combine the two basic kinds of order, chronological and subtopical. We can arrange them according to the way subtopics fit together. In most cases, the topic itself helps us decide which kind of order should dominate. For example, the need for more opportunities for women to participate in campus athletics is likely to require arrangement by subtopic; it is focused on the present. A section of the piece could be chronological—perhaps recent actions by the administration to help satisfy the need—but arrangement by subtopic would dominate. If the topic, though, is the growing need, the piece would lend itself to a chronological account, probably with the first few sentences focused on the present, then a flashback.

So, think of how words should fit together with a sentence, and then how sentences should fit together. All of this is based on your ability and willingness to organize words and material.

From Andre Fontaine (*The Art of Writing Nonfiction*, Crowell):

Most people don't act on the basis of things they perceive only with their minds. They react to things they *know* intellectually, intuitively, instinctually, as the result of an emotional conviction. The creative journalist involves these elements in his reader's personality; he knows that in doing it emotions are usually more reliable than intellect.

For example, everyone has read a straight newspaper story about a child being killed by a car:

"Susan York, 7, daughter of Mr. and Mrs. Samuel York of 327 Livingston St., was struck and killed yesterday afternoon when she ran in the path of a car driven by Charles Williamson, 42, 408 South George St."

Have you ever seen it happen? Have you seen the little body lying in the street, still and shockingly *wrong*, because a body doesn't belong in the middle of a street, which is for cars? And, like all bodies, it looks flat, empty, doll-like. And the face of the mother, who comes running out in a housedress and dirty sneakers she's been wearing to mop the kitchen floor, with none of her armor of makeup, and with her hair in rollers. And the way her face is stripped bare of the masks we all wear against the world as she kneels and picks up the child; the way disbelief, then shock, then flooding grief wash over her face so nakedly it is oddly embarrassing and you want to turn away from this too threatening emotion. And the dulled expression on the face of the man driving the car that hit the child as he gropes to comprehend this thing he has done.

The first you read and, unless you know the family, forget in ten minutes. In the second you live the tragedy. It lives with you for years, becomes a part of your view of life and very probably changes your own driving habits. The first is a typical newspaper story; it conveys information which you perceive intellectually. The second is creative journalism; it invokes your emotions, as fiction writers have been doing for centuries.

So, know what you want to do with a story; make it memorable because it deserves to be, or make it typical.

Advice from the experts. Take it to heart. Better yet, take it to your typewriter.

I've got a little list

A list does not necessarily an article make, of course. But it can.

Let me try one on you to summarize a few points.

A list of "remembers."

- There is no captive audience, the writer should remember, because there isn't. It's the writer's task to captivate.
- Your message is not a must, the writer also should remember, because it isn't. It's the writer's task to prove the message is a must.
- Clarity is next to godliness should be the writer's eleventh commandment. And that means words which mean to others what they mean to you, lots of simple sentences, and jargon-shorn prose.
- Think before you write. Gather facts before you write. Organize before you write. Writing is easier (hard as it always shall be) if an idea precedes research precedes structuring precedes writing.
- In structuring, consider whether you're covering what needs to be and cutting out the rest. Don't cover too much. The result is likely to be you're covering too little or you're covering incompletely.
- Know your audience. Your approach, your selection of material, your writing methods should depend on readership and what that readership is likely to accept.
- Strive for the conversational in your writing. Try to make it sound a bit like talk because people seem most comfortable with language used that way. It's not so hard to do if you listen to what you've written. If you listen rather than just look.
- Consider the first five to ten words and make them count. Consider the first sentence and make it count. Consider the first paragraph and make it count. Consider the lead so that it counts. It serves to establish the subject, first of all, but also to set the tone, to attract attention, and to guide clearly into what follows. All that.
- Perhaps the lead shouldn't be written first. Try a thesis first: a statement or short paragraph that in a nutshell tells what your article is about. Thesis usually follows lead in

a story structure. You can write it first, however, to make sure you do it at all, and to make the lead emerge from your struggling brain just a bit easier.
- People fall in love with people, not statistics. And that's worth remembering, too. Meaning that you shouldn't overload with figures but instead use those figures you do use creatively. Meaning also that stories with people in them tend to attract more than those without.
- And unless you interest your readers, why bother? Interest factors must be considered. People are interested in people (themselves and others), in what people do, in their problems, in their progress, in their triumphs and despairs, in their eccentricities, in their excellence, in their wants and needs, in their fame, in their world and universe as these relate to them.
- Select those nouns and verbs carefully for they will outdo any list of adjectives. Pliny the Elder did not say the earth is cruel and beneficent and harsh and soft and dark and light and hot and cold and so forth. He noted that "the earth, gentle and indulgent, ever subservient to the wants of man, spreads his walks with flowers, and his table with plenty; returns, with interest, every good committed to her care; and though she produces the poison, she still supplies the antidote; though constantly teased more to furnish the luxuries of man than his necessities, yet even to the last she continues her kind indulgence, and, when life is over, she piously covers his remains in her bosom." Sorry I extended this item, but really, truly, genuinely I'm not belaboring the point; that passage is beautiful, and, oh, what a point it makes.
- Yes, and it is through the noun and verb that you *show* your reader what you're writing of rather than just *tell*.
- Narration is a boon to audience enthusiasm if it's appropriate and well done.
- So is description.
- Narration and description can serve to explain and to argue. Effectively.
- Film, television, and life may work in jump cuts. Writing doesn't. Strive for flow. Your

reader should at all points know where he is and where he's been, with some hint at least of where he's going.

- Good grammar doesn't hurt.
- Correct spelling doesn't hurt.
- Proper punctuation doesn't hurt.
- Accuracy doesn't hurt.
- Write to stimulate your reader, not yourself.
- Add whatever you like to this list.

The art of friendly persuasion

The act of accepting a speaking engagement implies a certain commitment by the speaker. It means the speaker must understand the audience and what it is likely to accept. It means a sensitivity to the dynamics of the situation. It means having a sense of direction, of purpose. It means preparation.

The job of the speaker is to persuade an audience. The task may be to persuade the listeners to act on the speaker's advice. It may be merely persuading them to listen. But persuasion is the aim. And one persuades only by first reaching listeners and forcing them to listen.

Now, there's no chance for the speaker to force listening through whips and chains. Nothing like a truly captive audience exists. Even if people are physically locked in a room, their minds—thank the Lord—can escape. So, the speaker faces an increasingly difficult task of captivating the audience, or proving to that audience that *what* he has to say is worth accepting because *how* he says it is so captivating.

I say increasingly difficult task, and that it is. We are all jerked and bumped about by so much information and entertainment and distraction and just plain noise (musical and otherwise) that our systems get tired more easily. We find it harder to concentrate for any length of time. We find it difficult just to sit still as long as we used to.

So, there we are, sharing space in a room with a speaker who um-uhs through "It sure is a pleasure to be with you this noon. . ." and on into the murk of forensic tedium. The speaker's job, remember, is to persuade us. And, of course, he doesn't. He fails to achieve even the most basic speaker-audience relationship. He fails to translate hearing into listening. Hearing is purely physical, and that's likely to happen if acoustics are reasonable, the speaker gets sufficiently above the mumble level, and people in the audience have washed their ears. Listening, however, is mental and emotional. It requires involvement, and it is not too likely if the speaker doesn't have either the good sense or the courtesy to prepare what he has to say and how he will say it.

No, hearing doesn't change into listening when we hear, "It's a pleasure and a privilege to be here today to speak with you and to tell you, uh, about what I do, uh. My job, uh, is to promote the activities of our region's largest drug company, a distinguished one, uh, Pharmaceuticals, Incorporated. And it's, uh, a wonderful job, one that I've done, uh, for about ten years now, I guess. It's an exciting job, with different things, uh, happening every day. I'm, uh, never bored."

But by now, uh, the people at the Rotary or at Kiwanis or at the local church are bored and drifting fast. The speaker is saying nothing to them, and is doing so without energy, without conviction, without fire, without oomph, partially because he hasn't prepared, partially because he doesn't really have the confidence to carry out the assignment, and partially because he just doesn't know how to make it work.

But if the speaker had thought enough about the message, if he had sat down to write out what he wanted to say, if he then had worked on his performance (maybe with a friend not afraid to say, "Gee, Doug, where's your personality? You're so dreary. Get excited, will you!"), then boredom, like the bugs in an insecticide commercial, would have been bonked out or carried away.

He'd have moved to the front of the room with much more confidence—knowing the audience, knowing the geography of the room and the eccentricities of the microphone, knowing in his heart just what he means in the words he's written, knowing in his head enough of the speech for eye contact at appropriate places, knowing how he wants to interpret what he's going to say.

And then he'd begin, with a script and a smile, or sufficient notes and neighborly nod.

"The druggist is the heart of a community," he'd say. "Sometimes he's a heartbeat away from disaster.

"He is first aid and relief and shelves of magazines to experience and sun shields and beauty creams and bubble gum. The druggist sells directions and dreams.

"We could not exist without him. He could not exist without my company, Pharmaceuticals, Incorporated, which supplies the potions and the lotions that folks need and want.

"We'd all find it much harder to exist without the pioneering research that leads Pharmaceuticals toward new health solutions.

"I was in charge of press relations, working with newspapers and television, when we revealed the development of Coldstream. A blue sky day appropriately, almost symbolically.

"News to share that we'd found a medicine that would rid a person of cough caused by cold congestion. News that so many of us would be spared future discomfort.

"Now that's a job worth having. And let me tell you more about it, first, by recalling some of the events surrounding Coldstream. . . ."

We are right there with the speaker, probably, because he is there with us. He's paid us homage through preparation. And though he may not be the most glorious speaker in the world and he lacks the lilt of Richard Burton in his voice, we're listening.

We're listening because we can learn something. We're listening because he's going to provide us some entertainment through his re-creation of an exciting event. We're listening because he's much more apt to be involved in what he's saying because he's actually saying something.

Sure, the speaker must consider voice, the variety of tone and pace and volume and rhythm and emphasis, the deadening impact of reading as reading rather than reading as talking. But chances are, if he's feeling the message, and if he's thought out how he'd like to interpret that message (the way he would in the comfort of an informal chat with a friend), then he's going to escape the worst pitfalls of public speaking. He will not be the monotone. He will not be the monopace. He will not be the sing-song nonstylist. He will turn performer enough, himself enough, to complement a strong message and turn audience uninvolvement into involvement.

A good speech is first of all an idea. Then it must turn into effective language. Then it becomes performance. These together will result in sincerity, in conviction, in believability.

All it takes is preparation.

Ho hum et al

During the 1980 political campaign syndicated columnist David Broder reported on a Democratic fund-raiser. He wrote:

In the course of a misspent 20 years on the political trail, I have attended dozens of Democratic dinners, where the drunken din was such that no one, including the speaker, had any idea what was being said.

Hubert H. Humphrey had standard advice for other Democrats going to such notoriously besotted affairs as the Philadelphia or New Jersey dinners. "You say, 'Buzz-buzz-buzz-buzz-buzz—Harry S. Truman! Buzz-buzz-buzz-buzz-buzz—John Fitzgerald Kennedy!'" Humphrey advised. "And then you get the hell out of there before they start throwing rolls at each other."

Last Saturday night, I was at a Democratic dinner here where you could hear a pin drop. Sen. John C. Culver (D-Iowa), who is locked in a tough, close re-election campaign against Rep. Charles Grassley (R-Iowa), was winding up his speech to the party faithful in a rather remarkable way.

Instead of the standard Humphrey-style pep talk, he was talking about arms control and the importance of reviving—not discarding—the Strategic Arms Limitation Treaty with the Soviet Union. And he was doing it not by reciting data on warheads and throw weights, but by reading a Japanese woman's recollections of her experiences, as a young girl, on the day the first atomic bomb was dropped on Hiroshima.

Listening to the terrifying description of the effect of fire, blast and radiation on human flesh, written 30 years ago by that Japanese woman, now filling a basketball arena in the amplified voice of the former Marine and Harvard fullback, brought the hundreds of Democratic revelers to sudden silence—and full attention.

Culver understood his audience. He understood a change in the nature of that audience. He understood that beneath the revelry there was concern. He also, probably without knowing, followed the by-now-classic advice offered close to fifty years ago by Richard Borden in his book, *Public Speaking as Listeners Like It.* Borden emphasized the need for purpose in a speech, a purpose that should be evident to listeners from the beginning of a talk and throughout.

He theorized, rather sagaciously, that an audience comes to a speech with four succeeding reactions against which the speechwriter and the speaker must prepare:
(1) Ho hum
(2) Why bring that up?
(3) For instance?
(4) So what?

Ho hum. An audience usually isn't there to be unfriendly, but it isn't there bug-eyed eager either. In fact, it tends to be bored to begin with and to be increasingly bored as the speech continues. That feeling has to be countered. You need to arouse, to light an interest immediately, from the first sentence on.

So, you shouldn't say, "Safety experts are fearful of what a lifting of the 55-mile-per-hour speed limit might mean to the rate of accidents and fatalities. There's been talk of raising the limit back to 65." And so forth.

Instead, say: "Five hundred funerals a week focusing on 500 bodies in 500 coffins, shiny and new. Five hundred funerals you can count on. Five hundred extra funerals, the air around them burdened with the grief of loved ones left behind. That's the likely result if, as some government officials plan, the 55-mile-per-hour speed limit is raised once more by ten." And so forth.

Why bring that up? You must channel the story home, localize it, make it mean something to your listeners. "It doesn't always happen to others. The experts insist that statistical laws of averages put two or three of those filled coffins right here in this city." And so forth.

For instance. That's the "and so forth." "I know of someone you know who's been struck such a blow, a blow from a car, driven, pushed for speed so that it could not be stopped in time. A someone here. Her boy would be 15 now. He only got to seven. Mary Blaisdell remembers the night. . ." And so forth.

So what? Well, in this case, we've really answered reaction four. It's hard to say "So what" to grief. But here you should remind your listeners of the point you've been making all along. You ask for action. "Write. No, don't merely write. See your member of Congress—in his office—in her next community meeting. Put the pressure on." And so forth.

Senator Culver appears to have overcome Borden's lethargy quartet. His approach and manner, as David Broder described them, blew away all "ho hum." He understood, as do all good speakers along with their writers, that speech communication is a two-way process. You seek to elicit response. That requires enticement. That requires projecting yourself into other people's personalities, into their heads. That requires developing an empathy.

You help yourself by talking of issues which touch people's lives, like the safety of children and the saving of a world for today's children. Survival is not difficult to sell. Environment, home, family, food, jobs, comfort, self-improvement all strike the mind as important. And if you know how to get those topics to other people's minds via the heart, then empathy, involvement, meaningful reaction won't be hard to attain.

The sufferance of an audience is your primary concern. You cannot try to make an audience put up with, or worse yet, suffer. It will not permit you. At the very least, bored listeners will shut you off, out of their heads.

John Culver knew this. You probably know it, too, but do you always practice it? Best you do.

The writer looks at his speech: planning, organizing, outlining

The assignment was a speech for some of my favorite ladies, the members of the Chicago Drama League, all hundreds of them. A speech on New York's theatre season.

Now that's a big subject.

The research went on for a year. Pleasant research, granted, at least some of the time, but lots of it. Time-consuming research.

But research is not my subject. Planning is. Organizing. Outlining.

It helps to outline a speech, to give it a sense of direction even before the real writing begins. It helps when you're writing your own speech. It's even more useful when you write for someone else.

An outline gives the speaker-to-be at least the shape of the picture that later the words will paint. And how much better to provide that and thereby give the speaker an opportunity to suggest alterations before all those finely-crafted words are committed to paper and he says about them, "But that's not what I had in mind."

A lot less trauma the outline way.

Writing for myself it's not so critical, but it's helpful. The writing certainly becomes easier once a plan has been established.

Now, an outline is not merely a series of Roman numerals and capital letters to which have been appended some general topics. There needs to be some flesh on them thar bones. Some sub-items. Some examples of elaboration. Even some choice wording. All that together gives the speaker a solid notion of what you're about to do for him. He can react knowledgeably. He can accept or ask for changes, and you—the writer—will have expended far less time and energy.

Here's how I worked out my speech.

I gathered up all the saved programs, notes, and clippings, and counted. Forty plays seen and worth mentioning. Now how to bring all these together? No problem about the start; I had a socko beginning, having watched as bulldozers bulldozed those two historic theatres, the Morosco and the Helen Hayes, to make way for "progress," for a new hotel which Mayor Koch and company insist will revitalize Times Square. And to give myself a feel for the speech that was to follow, I'd just write a lead, an opening, at least in rough form:

A week ago today, in about an hour, a monstrous hydraulic destroyer called Godzilla struck the first available walls of the Morosco, that theatre in which seven Pulitzer Prize plays had premiered.

The crowd was shouting, let me tell you. "Don't do it. Don't do it!"

But Godzilla did it.

Colleen Dewhurst wept.

Superman wept. Yes, Christopher Reeves wept, and said, "It's increasingly a battle between artists and technology. We have to band together to insure that New York never becomes another Pittsburgh or Houston."

Well, Reeves and Joe Papp and Colleen Dewhurst and Tammy Grimes and Estelle Parsons and Celeste Holm and Treat Williams and Michael Moriarty and close to 170 others did band together, to get arrested.

For once a lead came easily. But what next? Forty plays. Oh inspiration, strike me, I said to myself. Help me organize.

And somehow, as with all writers, inspiration struck. Not grand, glorious inspiration, but the simple, acceptable sort.

To show that despite the destruction, there remains always an element of continuity in the theatre, I decided to make passing mention of the best of last season's shows which still is around, *Amadeus;* continuing quality with new cast. Quality as a thread of continuity. As *Amadeus* the previous season, so *Nicholas Nickelby* this year. The biggest of the shows, so an obvious way to get into the season's events.

Go into story about not wanting to go because of length, then getting so involved that (1) I didn't want a dinner break, and (2) I didn't want it to end. Worth more than $100. "Thanks for the memory." Mention rhubarb about Tonies: *Nickelby* so good that maybe it should get a special set of awards, thereby leaving room for other winners. Bunkum. If it's best, it's best.

Next section: the year's new musicals. *Dreamgirls* highly overpraised although Jennifer Holliday is super as the discarded Supreme. "How can she sing the way she sings eight times a week and still have a throat left?" *The First,* about Jackie Robinson, underpraised. *Joseph and His Technicolor Dreamcoat,* ''one of those shows for children of all ages, and I like being a child again.'' Briefly note others.

Turn to stars, this having been a season for stars and star vehicles. Discuss how most of them went wrong, at the very least selecting material not worthy of them.

Liz Taylor, in *The Little Foxes.* Quote critic John Simon: ''At 49, Miss Taylor is not yet ready for the legitimate theatre.''

Katharine Hepburn. ''Not an evening to remember, and it should have been.''

Claudette Colbert. Another trifle of a play.

Donny Osmond, in *Little Johnny Jones.* Closed on opening night. ''Maybe George M. Cohan should be remembered for Jimmy Cagney's electric performance. Forget this one.''

Cher, in *Come Back to the 5 and Dime, Jimmy Dean, Jimmy Dean.* Quote New York *Post* headline: ''It's 5 and Dime—and not Worth It.''

Faye Dunaway. Wasted. Mention that play was done in Chicago a couple of years ago.

Anne Bancroft and Max von Sydow. Wasted, but he can make the emptiest of lines sound earth shaking. Quote sample limp line.

Joanne Woodward as Candida. Unworthy of Shaw.

I realized that the speech was sort of organizing itself. I'd go from an unsuccessful revival of Shaw to a successful one, *Misalliance.* And I'd compare it to the wonderful version at Chicago's Academy Playhouse (play up local angle for Chicago people).

Othello. Tell how Giuseppe Verdi wanted to make Iago the central character of his opera. Tell story of Sir Donald Wolfit, the British actor who fired all his Iagos because no matter how bad they were, they seemed to get better notices than he as Othello, so he started to play Iago himself. Stress that the roles are unequal, and they remain so in this production, Christopher Plummer as the evil one getting the better of James Earl Jones as the good one.

Mention *King Lear* and the statuesque performance of Robert Stattel, who's not a tall man. His ''Lear can look in on himself and back on his life and know what has gone wrong and why. And in that lies tragedy.''

(It's useful, dear reader, to plug in those key phrases; that makes the writing easier later on.)

Touch on other revivals, most heavily on *My Fair Lady* and Rex Harrison's 25th anniversary as Higgins.

Then switch to our major younger dramatists:

John Guare. His *Lydie Breeze* a dud. Tell convoluted and inane plot.

Lanford Wilson's *A Tale Told.* Explain this is latest of his Talley family plays. Tie to Chicago productions.

Move further off Broadway:

(1) Bob Gunton. Identify him as the guy you see in all the *Evita* commercials; he's Peron. Now he's in a play that calls for him to do 20 roles. ''Count 'em. Twenty. And manic.''

(2) *Sister Mary Ignatius Explains It All for You.* The Christopher Durang play has more than a bit of venom in its satire.

(3) *Torch Song Trilogy,* a Harvey Fierstein ''extravaganza.'' He wrote the three one act plays, lasting more than four hours. And he stars in them. ''He's a first-rate playwright and a first-rate actor. What a combination.'' Tell situation of final play. Quote the lacerating humor of the Jewish mother and the gay son. Virtuosic.

(4) David Hwang's *Family Devotion.* The Chinese-American picture. A playwright to watch.

(5) Beth Henley. She's the southern-American. Her *Crimes of the Heart* did not deserve a Pulitzer, but still. . .

(6) *Snow Orchid.* Italian-American. Tough-to-take humor, but surprisingly, the play ends on upbeat. Mention Circle Rep and the other ''best'' theatre companies of the city.

Then wrap up other plays worth mentioning: *Mass Appeal, The Dresser,* Lena Horne, *Cloud Nine, Kingdoms, The Dining Room.* Stress performances and scenes.

End with most riveting scene of the season, from *Crossing Niagara.* Alvin Epstein as tight-rope walker losing his composure in mid-journey. Share choreography of that moment.

Conclude the speech, say that it's gone long, but then the season has had much worth mentioning. Let's see, I might say at the end:

The rest of *Crossing Niagara* isn't anywhere near that level of suspense and involvement. But that moment is a glory. And that's what theatre is all about: moments of glory, during which we forget who we are and where we are and when we are, and we enter another world that will tell us so much more, that will hold us tight and love us and move us and keep our minds rich with memories.

It is that way in New York as it is here in Chicago.

And it is love for that experience which has brought us together again this morning. For that I'm most grateful.

End. Now let's start writing.

Believe me, with such planning accomplished, a speech is considerably easier to write. Try it if you haven't. Continue to do so, if you have.

Beginnings: gaining admission

Here are some one-liners for your speech about the morality of business people:

When they say, "Good morning," we call the weather bureau to make sure.

They talk in stereophonic style—out of both sides of their mouth.

When they pat you on the back, they're trying to get you to cough up something.

Would you begin your speech with one or all of them? I wouldn't. I'd rather say:

Let me tell you of Jerry Hammill.

And of a family from Bridgeport he serves as insurance agent.

Yes, insurance agent. But listen.

The family suffered the agony of a father's grievously extended illness and then his death.

Jerry Hammill personally watched over that flock. The benefits from an income-loss policy were always at the house on time. He saw to that. He hand-delivered the checks.

And when the father died, those insurance benefits—so desperately needed—came quickly. He saw to that, too.

But Jerry Hammill did more. He also bought food, which was too scarce in the household. And he took the three youngest children to the movies and to church.

And he counseled.

A shortage of morality in business? Not so. Jerry Hammill proves it. As does a giant of a company like United Technology when it almost single-handedly saves the life of an opera company. . . .

You don't want to fall victim to the cliche. And the comedy beginning; the introduction tied to a pat set of jokes taken from a speechmaker's collection, is not the way to gain listener attention.

Your beginning should attract, startle, interest, intrigue. It should be fashioned for that occasion and that audience only. It should be custom-made.

As with anything you write—be it a news story or a magazine article or a novel or a speech—your lead, your start, your opening is most important. It gains you admission to your listener's brain. Or fails to. It involves the listener in what you're trying to get across to him. Or fails to. It persuades or inspires your listener to continue listening to what you've written or to act upon it. Or fails to.

So be creative.

Sure you can be funny if you've got the right kind of funny story and it fits the occasion. Or you can tug at the heart strings. Or you can set a scene:

The other day I bicycled home from the office, and there—in the sky—majestic, graceful—a bird sweeping, soaring.

A mammoth bird. And as I continued to watch, I realized it was the largest bird I'd ever seen. Like a pterodactyl almost, that flying dinosaur so long extinct. Far larger than a condor or eagle.

But there it was.

I stopped to get a better look.

And then I realized I must be dreaming. It wasn't a bird at all. It was a man, with wings.

And then you can go on to explain that, indeed, it was a man, but that the wings were not attached by nature, and that you weren't dreaming. It was real. The man was hang-gliding.

You can illustrate, too, as a student at Wisconsin State did some years ago in a speech on child adoption laws, a speech reprinted in *Winning Orations.* Gail Bauer wrote this to start her fine oration:

Picture this: a husband comes to the hospital to pick up his wife and new baby. As he passes the nursery door, he reads a sign which says: "Parents: No infants released until satisfactory answers can be given to these questions—Are you Catholic, Protestant, or Jew? Do both parents share the same faith? Do you belong to a church? Please name. Will the child receive religious training? Note: Non-believers need not apply."

An actual sign? Of course not. Incredible? Yes, for couples lucky enough to conceive and bear their own children. But for those who seek a child through adoption, these questions are no laughing matter. For in this land of religious freedom, the wrong religion, or—even worse—no religion, can be the bar between the happy union of a child who needs parents and a couple who want a baby to love.

A beautiful beginning. It would be hard for a listener to resist.

Sometimes you may just wish to get to the point quickly, and thereby startle your audience:

I'm going to ask you for money.

Now I could sing for you.

I could tell you jokes.

I could recite poetry.

I could circumnavigate and circumlocute.

I could even convolute.

And if you want me to, I will. But I'm really just going to ask for money.

Whatever way seems appropriate for the occasion, use that way to get your audience emotionally and intellectually. Arouse an interest immediately.

Reinforcing the message

When your favorite pro team makes a touchdown, goal, or basket, and the game is televised, then you rest assured that you can see the happy event again and again via instant replay. You get another chance at the missed quick shot. And even if you did see it the first time, the second look provides you with added satisfaction and closer scrutiny through slow motion or a picture taken from a different angle.

Instant replay makes sure you get the high point.

It works that way in speeches, too.

Consider the next one you write as a series of instant replays.

After all, you want the listeners to get the main point—to recognize it and to remember it. So why not do what the advertising folks do: (1) tell them what you're going to tell them; (2) tell them; (3) tell them what you told them.

Since there's no automatic, no televised instant replay of the touchdown you're trying to score with your speech, you have to build it in. Your task as speechwriter is to find ways to reinforce your message without suggesting to listeners that your talk is little more than repetition.

It really is a mistake to cover too much. Better to make that most important point well. For that to happen, reinforcement is necessary. If you use various informational techniques available to the writer—the narrative, the illustration, statistics, analysis, analogy—then the repetition will be barely noticeable. Your speech may even become more interesting to listen to.

Permit me to create portions of a speech for you.

To illustrate.

It happened in a movie house near New York's Plaza Hotel. On a weekday, late afternoon. I'd finished my business early and decided to see the Zeffirelli production of "Romeo and Juliet," a lovely film, perhaps not to Shakespeare scholars but for those, like me, who accept unusual interpretations of the great man's plays. . .if they work. This film worked for me. But the point of my story involves me less than others. In that audience was not one other adult. Only high school children. Inner city kids, I found out later. They came in like rowdies, ready for a noisy romp. Like most kids away from the classroom

for an afternoon. Why, I fretted, why must this happen to me? Can't I have a peaceful, quiet involvement with Shakespeare's glorious tragedy. Well, I needn't have feared. Those youngsters turned as quiet as I, except to cheer and shout and laugh and gasp at none but the appropriate moments. As the tale of Romeo and his Juliet unfolded once again, these young people were as moved as I, perhaps more. They left, no doubt, enriched.

A situation that tells me the arts are not fluff and flippery. They're not a tangent off to the edges of life's focus. And this even though some influential members of the new Administration seem to think so. In support of a call to slash the budgets of the arts and humanities endowments, the Administration says: "Given the need for reductions across the full range of Federal programs that meet more basic human needs, low priority items must bear a greater burden if fiscal restraint is to be achieved in a balanced and compassionate way."

"Programs that meet more basic human needs." "Low priority items." "Bear a greater burden."

Oh, I wish these new burocrats had been in that movie theatre with me. I wish David Stockman, the President's budget chief, had been there. Maybe then—in recognition of art's values—he'd change his thinking expressed in such declarations as the National Endowment for the Arts is not important, that it is insignificant and unnecessary.

The Arts Endowment last year received an appropriation of less than one dollar per person.

So, we're talking of symbolism to begin with. But the Arts Endowment has become important as symbol: a symbol that our nation's leaders care. To reduce that symbol, possibly to remove that symbol—an action that also has been proposed by some who have the ears of our new Administration—to reduce or remove that symbol is to diminish the perceived importance of the arts among too many of our people. And that's a tragedy you should not permit to happen.

We're underway. With example, with thesis, with a touch of statistics. The point of our speech has been introduced. Now is no time to leave it.

A government exists to serve.
Defense, ah yes.
Health and social welfare—well, maybe.
The arts—not important enough.

Well, I won't buy that notion. The arts are not unimportant. They can be, often are, and more often should be central to what we do and are. And as symbol and pump primer, the government can serve.

Who says the arts don't matter?

A school room in Streamwood, Illinois. A primary level reading class. Boys and girls seemingly riveted to their chairs, watching, listening. Watching several of their friends act out a little story about jelly beans and honesty. Listening to still another classmate read the story being performed. The teacher looks on. Another adult, an agile black man, suddenly bounds onto the stage, turning into an ogre cackling as he simulates a jelly bean grand theft.

Boos and hisses reverberate in the classroom, and laughter, too.

Says the teacher to me, an observer. "The boy who's reading. . .please consider that only three months ago he was refusing to read. He sat sullenly, silently. And now he's reading, and—as you can see—he's reading with feeling."

The reason: that agile black man—a member of Chicago's Free Street Theatre and a partially public funded program to teach reading by an alternative method: drama.

A child learning to read through theatre.

Who says the arts don't matter?

And while we're talking of youngsters, consider the competition sponsored by Pulitzer Prize winning poet Gwendolyn Brooks. A poetry contest for school children.

Abraham, a winner age 13, recites: "When I cannot hear birds while you can—you and these hearing people; hear all of the joy, while I don't. . .these chirps flew to your ear. Not to mine. Why?"

Abraham is deaf.

Ebony, age 8, writes: "My city is a junky city. Windows are dead about my head. Sometimes I cry when I look at the sky. Cause the world I wanted is dead in my hands."

The sociology of urban life—told in a little girl's artistry.

Who says the arts don't matter?

Through the oft-attacked Comprehensive Employment and Training Act—CETA—a school for the deaf in Falmouth, Maine, hires a painter-in-residence; guitarists work with pre-school youngsters at day care centers in Flint, Michigan; muralists paint pride and prowess onto building walls in New York City; a theatre troupe is sent to senior citizens homes in Denver.

Who says the arts don't matter? Who says government funding of those arts should be low priority? Not I, thank you. Not you, I hope.

You get the idea, I'm sure. Examples prove the point. The message gets reinforced. "Oh may it sink in," is the speaker's prayed-for expectation.

Low priority? Not meeting a basic human need? Well, 64 percent of our taxpayers suggest otherwise, if a poll is correct in which they indicate they'd gladly add five dollars to their tax burden to support the arts.

The previous funding level for the Arts Endowment—a bill over 150 million—amounts to less than a dollar a person, as I mentioned earlier. Actually less than 75 cents. Of the projected 700 billion dollar federal budget, that figure would be smaller than one/4,000th portion. One/4,000th!

At that level of 150 million, the cost of government support to the arts would be less than for three miles of road.

And they want to cut it in half?

Eliot Feld, the choreographer, suggests that instead of cutting the dance appropriation in that budget by five million dollars as contemplated, why not cut the length of five new nuclear submarines, each by a foot. After all—what's a foot to such a juggernaut of underwater power?

Statistics have moved into the speaker's arsenal of arguments. It's time now to bring matters to a close. And maybe, we should turn to authority and heart-felt grandstanding.

Pollster Lou Harris, advocate for the arts, has said: "We do not build monuments nor functional widgets. We only affect the psyche; we only uplift the spirit; we only give people a chance to reflect on life; we only provide fleeting moments of positive and joyous experience as a respite from the worries over the excesses of inflation, pressures and anxieties from an ever-increasingly

91

complex world we live in, from concerns over-wars and taxes. . . .Perhaps we are only a small refuge in a wilderness of discontent. But perhaps our collective effort is much more. Perhaps we provide those magical moments that our people do not forget. Perhaps our contributions are close to the heart of what makes the rest bearable.''

The words of Lou Harris, pollster and lover of the arts.

Oh, if the would-be cutters of budget would but listen.

The author of "Ragtime," E.L. Doctorow, appeared recently before a Congressional subcommittee hearing testimony on the proposed cuts. He told the legislators that the cuts when placed alongside massive increases in defense spending advance the notion, as he put it, of "the sovietizing of American life, building a vast armory, but with nothing but emptiness inside.

Soprano Leontyne Price sang her testimony. To

Irving Berlin's "God Bless America":

Save the performing arts,
Arts that I love.
Stand beside us,
And guide us,
Through the night with
Those funds from above.
From the mountains
To the prairies
To the oceans white with foam,
Please save the performing arts.
Don't let us fall.

Miss Price was greeted with a standing ovation.
Let's hear it for her and for her beloved arts.
Our arts.

Now, you write about your pet project, your philanthropy, your object of advocacy. Make that point, and make it again and again. It's a matter of reinforcing your message through self-provided instant replay.

Tell 'em three times

I've written of this before, but it cannot be overstressed.

Just recently I sat among the unfortunate listening for more than an hour to a top executive attempting to marshal his troops for a more glorious corporate tomorrow. Present conditions were somewhat financially depressed, and therefore depressing; his purpose was to uplift and to stir his people to greater effort.

A laudatory aim.

But the man droned, which was no help.

And the man presented a speech so fully stuffed that to a listener it proved indigestible.

Not only did he (and his speechwriter) strive to urge renewed vigor in work patterns, but he (1) recounted in seemingly endless statistics (all with obtuse slides, of course) the 75-year economic history of the company; (2) reviewed acquisitions and de-acquisitions through all those years; (3) shared several organizational plans (and quite honestly I cannot tell you if they dealt with past and/or present and/or future; I do know I couldn't figure out all the lines and boxes and arrows and whatsits on another series of slides); (4) talked of space; (5) mentioned salaries and benefits; (6) introduced members of the board of directors—and this, for some strange reason, in the middle of the speech, and (7) opined on Reaganomics and the American economy.

It was positively stupifying, not only to me (and I was merely an onlooker) but to the troops. Vacant stares, closed eyelids, even nodding heads toward the rear could be spotted despite the dusky light.

The executive attempted to say too much, to cover more than he need have or should have.

His main point was to inspire his colleagues. That's all he should have done. The rest of the material was ripe for handouts. "What I'm urging you to do is work harder, and I'll tell you why. But to provide additional context, permit me to hand out some printed material which deals with history and philosophy and economy. You'll find it supports and explains what I most want to share with you today."

That would have reached more receptive folks. The offending executive should have heeded a lesson from advertising professionals who seek assurance that a commercial message reaches its intended audience.

Really reaches it.

Seeps in.

They don't cover too much. They're satisfied with the successful communication of *one* message per ad. And they use the technique of instant reminders, so that in a reader's quick perusal of an ad, somehow he or she gets the point, that *one* message.

I've mentioned the method before:
(1) Tell 'em what you're gonna tell 'em.
(2) Tell 'em.
(3) Tell 'em what you told 'em.

It's done so carefully, with such refinement— at least in the best ads—that the reader isn't aware of the repetition at work on his mind.

This is a useful technique for the speechwriter.

We've learned that listeners can accept only so much. Good speechwriters know it. They reject the once more commonly held notion that a speech should be packed with points. Of course one shouldn't waste a listener's time; he should benefit from the listening. But comfort should be built in, too, the comfort of an informational pacing that ears and mind can accept.

A point well made is a speech well made. Five points hazily made are a speech hazily made. The listener is likely to forget what was said.

So, build your speech on the advertising formula. Introduce your point, as engagingly as possible. Then expand on it with additional engagingly enlightening information. Then summarize the message to pass it by the auditor once again.

And maybe, just maybe, well, more likely than maybe, the point will have been made.

Creative repetition wins you followers.

Let's say you wish to speak about the importance of higher education for blacks, the availability of educational opportunity to blacks, the concern about too many young blacks being deprived and therefore falling victim to unemployment or at least underemployment, and what this does to family and pride and hope and neighborhood, and how because of all this the whole society suffers.

Granted, all those topics are really one in that they merge, one into the other, one from the other. But a writer must find a way of funneling the ideas through one main point, one recommendation which, if followed, may cause a move away from deprivation.

Let's tackle the problem through a plea to support predominantly black institutions of higher learning, this through the Negro College Fund. "You may think," I'd begin:

. . .those street-oriented young blacks don't care, that they're satisfied lounging and congregating for noisy small talk on street corners and available stairs, that the disco and a general aimlessness are a preferred way of life.

Bunk!

It's only your perception, if that's what you think. It's only your failure to understand that hope too oft and too long denied alters into despair, or at least an "I give up because no one's gonna help me."

I've talked to these youngsters. They have a bitter edge to their words, some of them. And their body language, which may on casual study suggest swagger and strut and shoulder sway, a coolness and control, turns out to be—believe me—defensive posture, a mask intended to cover fear and even grief.

It isn't fair to burden our young people—any of them—with fear and grief.

It isn't fair to let bright thoughts, and believe me once again, these youngsters are bright—it isn't fair to let bright thoughts go undeveloped and unused.

There are schools for these young people, schools that want them and will train them, schools that need all of us to help.

The Negro College Fund needs you because

thousands of teenagers need what that fund can pay for.

That's the message of your talk. Then comes justification, all to make the point sink in.

Talk of the increasing flow of black teenagers who could benefit from the education. Statistics.

Talk of the educational excitement on the campuses. Examples. Anecdotes. Description.

Talk of a young man who couldn't attend because the school he wanted and that wanted him didn't have enough financial aid to take care of his needs. Talk of a young woman who lost out because the school she could attend had to cut budget and enrollment. Personal experiences. Narratives.

Talk about former students, graduates of the colleges who are succeeding as doctors and engineers and teachers and psychologists and journalists and singers because they had the opportunity. Examples.

Talk in summary of the rickety state of some colleges in these troubled years, of the threat and the promise, of what ignoring the youngsters means to them and to neighborhood and to country, of what helping is likely to accomplish.

"A mind is too good a thing to waste."

And with that well-known motto, stop.

You've probably covered all that you wanted to say, but in a manageable configuration. All your concerns have been compressed into one, a concern which you've stated and restated and restated again, all to make sure that the listening turns into action.

Tell 'em.

Tell 'em.

Tell 'em.

The motivated sequence

You've heard, no doubt, of the motivated sequence, a method of structuring speeches designed to motivate listeners to action, to persuade. Alan Monroe and Douglas Ehninger, professors of speech, are credited with its development.

Many gifted speakers have used it and continue to.

Here's how it works:

(1) You gain the listener's *attention* with something pertinent that startles.

(2) You show the *need* for an action or course you're about to recommend.

(3) You explain how the need can be *satisfied* through your proposal.

(4) You *visualize* the improvement or change or solution that will result from your recommendations.

(5) You ask for approval or *action*.

It's a classic format by now, easy for the writer to structure, easy for the listener to follow. And if you take full advantage of the format—that is through the use of illustrations and pointed statements and personal experiences and narrative examples and descriptive highlights—you can get your message across successfully and easily.

Let's say you're addressing fellow citizens at the town hall, urging support for a bond issue, one that was defeated in a previous vote.

Attention:

I've brought no dancing girls. I've no jokes to share with you. You know why you're here and why you should listen. The welfare of your children, the maintenance of property values. Serious business.

So let me give you numbers. Twelve. Eighteen. Twenty-five.

Twelve. A twelve percent increase in property damage incidents.

Eighteen. An 18 percent increase in burglaries.

Twenty-five. A 25 percent increase in vandalism.

All these in the past six months. All these since three out of every four street lights were turned off, since night recreation facilities were closed, since YMCA operations ceased.

Need:

I won't say I told you so.

But I will remind you of a scene probably all too familiar. Your teenager says to you, "Mom, Dad, I'm going out." So you ask: "To do what?" And the answer comes back, "Oh, I don't know. Just hang out."

Hang out where? That's the question and the problem. Let's face it, friends, without the teen dancing and rollerskating at the Y, without the gym and pool and ice rink at the high school, there's little our youngsters can do after sundown. Little, that is, in a healthy environment. The churches and synagogues are trying to fill the nighttime gap, but they just can't do it alone.

Satisfaction:

Last week our township administrator estimated the cost to you of putting the lights back on and restoring life to our community after sundown. That cost: 43 dollars per family per year.

Are your kids worth 43 dollars?

On November 3rd, please put politics aside. Vote on the merits of the referendum. You have a chance to right a wrong.

Visualization:

For those of you who say, "What's in it for me?" or "I have only pre-schoolers" or "My children are long out of the nest," so "Why should I spend an extra 43 dollars per year?"—well, I can only respond that not to do so is to be penny wise and pound foolish, and let cliches fall where they may.

When you bought your home here, did you ask the real estate agent about recreational facilities available for the kids? Certainly. And you heard about playgrounds and ballfields and tennis courts and so forth, all usable day and night. That was a plus, I'm sure, as you determined the pluses and minuses of the contemplated purchase. You probably asked about crime rates. And when the agent said, "Oh, you can count the number of crimes committed around here in a year on two hands," you felt good about that and put down another plus.

But today it would take fingers on the hands of a centipede to count the crimes. And it would take a bat's vision to make use of our tennis courts.

Tomorrow you may want to sell your home. What are you going to tell prospective buyers? Honestly, I mean.

Action:

Let's turn the lights on again all over our world.

It's good for our children. It's good for us.

We're not asked too often to stand up and be counted. Indeed, too often we think, "What difference does my one vote make? I'll just skip being counted, or avoid it."

Well, the last time around the margin of defeat was 65 votes.

You should stand up and be counted. You must.

For the cost of a Saturday night dinner for two you can help preserve the well-being of your family and maintain the value of that most valuable financial asset, your home.

It's up to you. Turn those lights on, please.

The point is introduced, made, remade, and potentially sold.

The motivated sequence. A good way to persuade.

Words that rouse or rally

It's said that what you say first and last hold most importance in a speech. The beginning gains the speaker admission into minds. The ending is what those minds take with them.

If anything is remembered, it's the ending.

So the writer shouldn't waste the challenge.

An ending should ring verbally.

An ending should remind the listener what most you want to remind him of.

An ending should bring the speech to emotional as well as factual completion.

An ending should create a mood that lasts way beyond the talk itself.

I believe Vernon Jordan did all this when, in addressing the AFL-CIO, he finished with these words:

Many years ago, Samuel Gompers was asked— what does labor want?

What does labor want?

He replied: "We want more school houses and less jails, more books and less arsenals, more learning and less vice, more leisure and less greed, more justice and less revenge; in fact, more of the opportunities to cultivate our better natures, to make manhood more noble, womanhood more beautiful, and childhood more happy and bright."

And that, my brothers and sisters of the great American labor movement, is what black people want.

Jordan employed an oft-used yet effective technique: the quote. Lots of speakers before us created words so beautifully fused that it's a shame not to use them again (with credit, of course). Jordan did. You can.

Jordan's thoughts, as first expressed by Gompers, gave his listeners much to think about. They summarized his point. And in a way they were an appeal, a call to action. By using the words of one of theirs, Jordan most likely added to the force of his appeal. It's that sort of combination, the result of a carefully thought out approach, that makes listeners go out inspired or happy or angry or ready to fight or ready to spread brotherhood or whatever was the purpose of speechwriter and speechmaker.

Why, even Frederick the Great did that. Before the Battle of Leuthen in 1757 he told his officers:

The calvary regiment that does not on this instant, on orders given, dash full plunge into the enemy, I will, directly after the battle, unhorse and make it a garrison regiment. The infantry battalion which, meet with what it may, shows the least sign of hesitancy, loses its colors and its sabers, and I cut the trimmings from its uniform! Now, good night, gentlemen: shortly we have either beaten the enemy, or we never see one another again.

They saw each other again.

Churchill called his people to action repeatedly in dark hours of war, but never more potently than after the fall of France. "The Battle of Britain is about to begin," he said, and

On this battle depends the survival of Christian civilization.

Upon it depends our own British life and the long continuity of our institutions and our empire. The whole fury and might of the enemy must very soon be turned upon us. Hitler knows he will have to break us in this island or lose the war.

If we can stand up to him, all Europe may be freed and the life of the world may move forward into broad, sunlit uplands; but if we fail, the whole world, including the United States and all that we have known and cared for, will sink into the abyss of a new dark age made more sinister and perhaps more prolonged by the lights of a perverted science.

Let us therefore brace ourselves to our duty and so bear ourselves that if the British Commonwealth and Empire last for a thousand years, men will still say, "This was their finest hour."

Lord, if someone could speak to us today in such phrases—and with the fervency Churchill poured into the reading—we might actually be taunted to action—against poverty, for greater productivity, against violence, for energy conservation.

Churchill was a phrase maker. And if you can coin a phrase, don't hesitate. Your choice of words. Your own "Hunger knows no boundaries" and "A mind is too good a thing to waste" can become a battle cry for those to whom your speech is addressed.

A quieter, longer battle was Susan B. Anthony's

concern when in 1873 she pleaded for woman's suffrage:

> Webster, Worcester, and Bouvier all define a citizen to be a person in the United States, entitled to vote and hold office.

> The only question left to be settled now is: Are women persons? And I hardly believe any of our opponents will have the hardihood to say they are not. Being persons, then, women are citizens; and no State has a right to make any law, or to enforce any old law, that shall abridge their privileges or immunities. Hence, every discrimination against women in the constitutions and laws of the several States is today null and void, precisely as is every one against negroes.

There is education in Anthony's conclusion, a reminder of what terms mean and therefore what laws should mean.

A lesson shared can be a telling end. Socrates proved that, when he responded to his condemnation to death. He insists he bears no resentment, and then he adds:

> Thus much, however, I beg of them. Punish my sons, when they grow up, O judges, paining them as I have pained you, if they appear to you to care for riches or anything else before virtue, and if they think themselves to be something when they are nothing, reproach them as I have done you, for not attending to what they ought, and for conceiving themselves to be something when they are worth nothing. If ye do this, both I and my sons shall have met with just treatment at your hands.

> But it is now time to depart—for me to die, for you to live. But which of us is going to a better state is unknown to everyone but God.

You'll note in all these how important is language, that memorable way to say a memorable thing. You'll note in most that the speaker summarizes or reviews the major point. You'll note in those where action should follow that action is likely to because of words that rouse or rally.

Perhaps, however, you merely want to leave a picture behind, as did Mark Twain to the New England Society of New York City. His topic was New England weather, a subject he had introduced with, "I reverently believe that the Maker who made us all, makes everything in New England—but the weather." He finishes with these words:

> If we had not our bewitching autumn foliage, we should still have to credit the weather with one feature which compensates for all its bullying vagaries—the ice storm—when a leafless tree is clothed with ice from the bottom to the top—ice that is as bright and clear as crystal; every bough and twig is strung with ice-beads, frozen dewdrops, and the whole tree sparkles, cold and white, like the Shah of Persia's diamond plume. Then the wind waves the branches, and the sun comes out and turns all those myriads of beads and drops to prisms, that glow and hum and flash with all manner of colored fires, which change and change again, with inconceivable rapidity, from blue to red, from red to green, and green to gold; the tree becomes a sparkling fountain, a very explosion of dazzling jewels; and it stands there the acme, the climax, the supremist possibility in art or nature of bewildering, intoxicating, intolerable magnificence! One cannot make the words too strong.

> Month after month I lay up hate and grudge against the New England weather; but when the ice storm comes at last, I say: "There, I forgive you now; the books are square between us; you don't owe me a cent; go and sin some more; your little faults and foibles count for nothing; you are the most enchanting weather in the world!

Now there's something to take away with you. Words. Wonderful words.

Whether you provide such an illustration or a quote or a pithy summary or a ringing call to the struggle, your aim should be to be memorable.

As Mark Twain was.

And I am not.

Read aloud what you write

Too many speechwriters don't bother to read aloud what they've written for themselves or their clients. And without doing that, the writer cannot know the cadences and sound combinations work.

It is not enough, of course, for the writer to provide good information and well-crafted verbiage. That information, that verbiage must sound good. And for that to happen, the words must flow comfortably from the speaker's mouth.

Here's a sentence that's perfectly acceptable in terms of structure and readability (on paper, that is):

In such a dynamic environment, the central question is "How can we create a system that guarantees that our knowledge and detection of potential health risks are translated into practicable guidelines to assure employee and public safety?"

Try reading that aloud. Try breaking it into patterns that flow. Try breathing yourself through it. Difficult. What to do?

In this dynamic environment, we have to ask ourselves some questions. How can we translate what we know about potential health risks into language people can understand? How can we create practical, usable guidelines to assure employee and public safety?

The writer must help the speechmaker, not hinder him.

Sentence structure, if clear and simple, can help. Prounounceable words can help ("conflagration", "synthesis", "carcinogenesis" are not helpful words). A flow from sentence to sentence can help.

But, of course, structure is only part of the problem. The writer also must build into his work the kind of language, the kind of approach, the kind of informational techniques that are going to help the speaker get major points across.

I suspect the possibilities are infinite.

Let me just suggest a few, which perhaps you've used, but which really aren't used often enough.

Quotes, strong quotes, telling quotes can be useful. They tend to perk the listener. They give a good speaker an opportunity to play with interpretation. And, oh, how they can impress us with a point. Take Robert H. Jackson's conclusion to his speech before the tribunal trying the Nazis for their war crimes, this back in 1945. Notice how he builds toward a quote, how that quote stresses his message, and how Jackson comes out of it:

When for years they have deceived the world, and masked falsehood with plausibilities, can anyone be surprised that they continue the habits of a lifetime in this dock? Credibility is one of the main issues of this trial. Only those who have failed to learn the bitter lessons of the last decade can doubt that men who have always played on the unsuspecting credulity of generous opponents would not hesitate to do the same now.

It is against such a background that these defendants now ask this Tribunal to say that they are not guilty of planning, executing, or conspiring to commit this long list of crimes and wrongs. They stand before the record of this trial as bloodstained Gloucester stood by the body of his slain King. He begged of the widow, as they beg of you: "Say I slew them not." And the Queen replied, "Then say they were not slain. But dead they are. . ."

If you were to say of these men that they are not guilty, it would be as true to say there has been no war, there are no slain, there has been no crime.

In a different way I made use of another person's verbal gifts in a talk about the importance of the arts by introducing one Charles Doss into my discussion. Doss had turned to writing, I told my audience, while he was on death row in the Arizona State Prison. He had decided to compose poetry as a way to keep his head straight and as a form of repentence. I said:

A poet born on death row. A poet who vowed to write 2-thousand poems before death.

He writes beautifully, with love in his heart and verbal agility at his command. One of Charles Doss' sonnets is called Pulsations.

"Sometimes this prison womb her ebb and flow
Upon my breast impresses
Until I seem to catch a sound that comes
From distant universes.

"It is a wild, majestic crash, as if
Exploding nebulae
Were bridging all of space with messengers
Their language to convey

"And neither verb it has, nor adjective,
But such a mighty Noun
That it shall permeate this dungeon when
These bars have lost their fame.

"The noun is *peace,* and in the prison hush
My soul grows giddy with its madding crash!"

The power of art. The need for art. To this man
the art of poetry is everything.

I should tell you that Doss had his sentence
commuted to life. He continues to write poetry.

Rhetorical devices belong to the speechwriter's
arsenal of methods, too. You'll recall Martin
Luther King, Jr.'s "I have a dream" speech, a
brilliant example of repetition for emphasis.
Franklin D. Roosevelt liked to use repetition; he
did so in several of his most important speeches.
Take this, from his second inaugural address
in 1937:

Here is the challenge to our democracy: In this
nation *I see* tens of *millions* of its citizens—a
substantial part of its whole population—who at
this very moment are denied the greater part of
what the very lowest standards of today call the
necessities of life.

I see millions of families trying to live on incomes
so meager that the pall of family disaster hangs
over them day by day.

I see millions whose daily lives in city and on farm
continue under conditions labeled indecent by a
so-called polite society half a century ago.

I see millions denied education, recreation, and
the opportunity to better their lot and the lot of
their children.

I see millions lacking the means to buy the
products of farm and factory and by their poverty
denying work and productiveness to many other
millions.

I see one-third of a nation ill-housed, ill-clad,
ill-nourished.

It is not in despair that I paint you that picture. I
paint it for you in hope—because the Nation,
seeing and understanding the injustice in it,
proposes to paint it out. . . .

What power in that repeated phrase. And just
read Roosevelt's words out loud. See how
beautifully they read.

One can achieve attention (and added credibility) by calling upon the recognized authorities,
Jackson Browning, the corporate director of
health, safety, and environmental affairs for
Union Carbide, did even better than that while
addressing the Chemical Manufacturers Association in Atlanta last year. He called upon irony
and surprise in his use of authority:

I'd like to begin addressing the very pressing and
volatile issue of hazardous waste disposal by
thanking some of the people who have made it
necessary for us to be here: Rachel Carson, Bob
Dylan, Ralph Nader, Richard Nixon, and Douglas
Costle. I've left out a good many, I know, but
there isn't time to thank everyone.

The immediate impression is, "Hm. Just as
one would expect from an executive of the
chemical industry. The usual attack, with a
twist." But, no, the twist is of another sort.
Here's how Browning continues:

I note Rachel Carson because, until she wrote
"Silent Spring" in the sixties, most Americans
were blissfully unaware of dangers to the environment from chemicals and wastes.

Bob Dylan, because of his memorable song that
said, "You know that something's happening, but
you don't know what it is, do you, Mr. Jones?"
That has proven to be prophetically true about a
number of issues, not least of which is the one
we're concerned with today.

Ralph Nader, because he mobilized the first
effective and broadly-based mass environmental
movement; Richard Nixon, because he signed the
law that created the Environmental Protection
Agency just ten years ago; and Douglas Costle,
the administrator of EPA, because he bears the
responsibility today of taking concrete action to
deal with these complex concerns

Devils have become angels, and Browning has
sided with them. The argument that follows is
bound to be stronger.

So many ways. As speechwriter it's your job to
find the way that imprints a message on the audience. Style you should call upon. Techniques

you should call upon. And take time to read other people's speeches, that way to inspire yourself. As I did recently the 1850 message "to the Great Chief at Washington" from Hiamovi, the Cayenne and Dakota Indian Chief:

I want all white men to read and learn how the Indians lived and thought in the olden time, and may it bring holy-good upon the younger Indians to know of their fathers. A little while, and the old Indians will no longer be, and the young will be even as white men. When I think, I know that it is the mind of the Great Mystery that white men and Indians who fought together should now be one people.

There are birds of many colors—red, blue, green, yellow—yet it is all one bird. There are horses of many colors—brown, black, yellow, white—yet it is all one horse. So cattle, so all living things—animals, flowers, trees. So men: in this land where once were only Indians are now men of every color—white, black, yellow, red—yet all one people. That this should come to pass was in the heart of the Great Mystery. It is right thus. And everywhere there shall be peace.

Someone wrote down the Chief's words, but you know as I know that he said them out loud.

Here's how the speechwriter put it

The latter question, certainly not devoid of very important connections to the first, is partly the subject of my remarks today.

Before I proceed with that discussion—namely, the policies and programs our nation has laid down to build a broader industrial base, and what the national bodies we have created for this purpose have achieved—allow me to set the stage with a few bubble-bursters related to my remarks above:

The drop in oil prices which has led to a stabilization in world inflation, much heralded by the Western press, could also cause further tightening in international lending, especially to the more impoverished countries of the Third World.

He wrote it that way. He certainly could not have spoken it that way. Meaning: he failed to read his copy out loud to test its talkability, its read-aloudability, its conversationality.

I edited, attempting to retain the essence of the message while making the words easier to speak:

It's that second question—relating to Saudi Arabia's quest for new economic directions—that I'd like to discuss with you today.

But permit me—in an aside—to suggest also that the drop in oil prices—though it has helped stabilize world inflation—could in addition cause further tightening in international lending, especially to the more impoverished countries of the Third World.

The rewrite says the same thing. It's shorter and simpler.

And a bit later the speechwriter wrote:

Now having set the stage as I promised, let me begin my formal remarks by reiterating the long-sought goal of Saudi Arabia. We are firmly committed to, and in no way altered by recent events, to the total economic diversification of the Kingdom. It is our nation's overriding economic policy to pursue industrial diversification utilizing the resources afforded by oil revenues.

Recent events demonstrate all too well, however, why this goal grows more important each day.

The edit altered the passage to read:

Now let me turn to Saudi Arabia's long-sought goal. We are firmly committed to—and that

commitment is in no way altered by recent events—to the total economic diversification of the Kingdom. We will pursue industrial diversification using the resources made possible by oil revenue. We will do so because we must do so for the continuing good of our people.

The job of the speechwriter is not merely to verbalize the thoughts of his speaker but to fashion language that the speaker can handle. Every speaker has strengths and weaknesses, words easily spoken and not so, sentence structures easily mastered and not so. But the simpler words usually work better. So do simple sentences, short ones.

You'll find out if you try your copy by reading it aloud. You'll also notice where the copy flows and where it doesn't. Flow is essential for copy that's to be listened to. You must avoid jump-cuts. A listener must know every moment where he is in a speech and where he's going, where he is now and where he's just been. Sentence should lead comfortably to sentence and paragraph to paragraph. Just the addition of a word or phrase or the twist of a sentence can cause that flow. Take this selection from another writer:

Ours is a society that possesses only two natural resources: our oil and our people. In forty years, more or less, our oil will run out. Our people will have to depend on their skills and productivity to earn a living.

Oil revenues are a wonderful blessing. But they are not real wealth. They are only the investment capital we can use to build real wealth.

The blessing of our oil revenues presented us with two choices: we could have determined that our income from oil made us a rich society, or we could appreciate the fact that our oil revenues only gave us the opportunity to become a rich society.

Only small changes were required for that passage, but those changes can make a difference.

Ours is a society that possesses only two natural resources: our oil and our people. In forty years, more or less, our oil will run out. What then for our other resource, our people? We cannot wait for then: so we have determined.

Oil revenues are a wonderful blessing. But they're

not real wealth. They're only the investment capital we can use to build real wealth.

We saw beyond the immediate blessing of our oil revenues and realized that oil revenues rather than making us a rich society only give us the opportunity to become a rich society.

Add the phrase or sentence that attaches one paragraph to another. "And that means." "Here's how it would work." "In addition." "But to look at it another way." "The choice was not difficult to make. The challenge was how." "Let me emphasize that."

Add the sentence that recapitulates succinctly what you've been talking about. "All that to encourage trade and investment." "We must not miss that opportunity."

Just make sure that the language can be talked (and don't forget contractions) and that the listener can stay with what you've written, can follow it easily.

To test what you've done: listen.

Indeed, if you can read your script into a tape recorder, set the script aside, and just listen, you'll become super-critical of what you hear. The result is likely to be a much more readable, more talkable speech. A much better speech.

Uses and abuses

Big long words name little things.
All big things have little names
Such as life and death, peace and war
Or dawn, day, night, hope, love, home.
Learn to use little words in a big way.
It is hard to do,
But they say what you mean—
Use big words.
That often fools little people.

—Arthur Kudner

About-Around
About means approximately. Around means starting at one point and coming back to that same point.

Accept-Except
Accept: to receive or take something that is offered.
Except: (1) to take out or leave out anything; (2) otherwise or other than.

Accord-Award
Accord: agreement
Award: give or honor given

Adapt-Adopt
When you adopt a child, you take the child as your own. It means to take as your own what was originally not your own. You cannot adopt yourself. But you can adapt yourself because adapt means to adjust yourself to new conditions.

Admission-Admittance
Admittance is used almost always in the sense of being allowed to enter. Admission means (1) a fee paid for being allowed to enter; (2) the act of being received or being allowed to enter a group, society, or school; and (3) owning up to an accusation or statement.

Affect-Effect
Affect: to influence, to impress. It is always a verb.
Effect: can be both noun and verb. As a noun it means (1) a result or consequence or outcome; (2) fulfillment or accomplishment;

(3) the making of an impression. As a verb it means to bring about, to execute.

Aggravate-Provoke
Aggravate: to make worse
Provoke: to arouse

Agree-Admit
Agree: concord
Admit: confess

Allege-Assert
Allege: formal charge
Assert: say

Allude-Elude-Refer
Allude: indirect mention or reference
Elude: slip away from
Refer: direct mention

Allusion-Illusion-Delusion
Allusion: indirect reference
Illusion: deceptive appearance
Delusion: false belief

Altogether-All together
Altogether: completely
All together: as all in one room

Among-Between
General rule is that between is used with two persons or things; among is used with three or more persons or things. A similar relationship exists between alternative and choice: alternative offers two courses of action, choice any number.

Amount
Applies to mass or bulk, not to number.

Anxious-Desire
Anxious: worried
Desire: wish

Anybody
Written as one word it means any person. Anybody means any corpse or any human form or any group. Same rule holds true for everybody, nobody, somebody.

Anyone
One word. If written "any one" might mean any single person or any single thing.

Apt-Likely-Liable
Apt: gifted
Likely: probably
Liable: exposed

As good or better than
Rearrange the sentence. Instead of saying: "My opinion is as good or better than his," say "My opinion is as good as his, or better (if not better)."

As to whether
Whether is sufficient.

At
Not to follow where. (Incorrect: "Where is your luggage at?"

Audience-Spectators
Audience: at concert or play—listeners
Spectators: witnesses at a tournament

Avocation-Vocation
Avocation: that which calls one away from one's vocation; a minor or subsidiary occupation, a by-work.
Vocation: one's occupation, work, or employment.

Bad-Badly
Bad is an adjective with various applications: a bad man, a bad cold, a bad night, a bad accident, bad weather, bad news, bad light, bad taste. Badly can be an adjective (I feel badly) or an adverb. Actually in the sentence above it is a predicate adjective, that is, it (badly) follows a linking verb (feel)—a verb that means little without a qualifier.

Beside-Besides
Beside means at the side of. Besides means in addition to.

Born-Borne
Correct uses are: "He was born on the first day

of the year," and "He was borne by his mother after three hours of labor."

Bravery-Courage
Bravery: inner quality
Courage: act of will

Bring-Take
Bring is the opposite of take. Bring means "to carry, to come with something toward the speaker or listener." Take means "to carry something away from."

But
Unnecessary after doubt and help. (Incorrect: "I have no doubt but that. . ." and "He would not help but see that. . ." Correct: "I have no doubt that. . ." and "He could not help seeing that. . .")

Can-May
Can: ability
May: permission

Can't hardly
Double negative. Correct: can hardly or can scarcely.

Capacity-Ability
Capacity: potentiality
Ability: faculty

Capital-Capitol
Capital refers to the city, the seat of government (Paris is the capital of France). It also means punishable by death—a capital crime. Capitol is a building where a legislature meets.

Certainly
Used indiscriminately by some writers, much as others use very; this is an attempt to intensify any and every statement.

Character
Frequently a redundant word. Such as: "Acts of a hostile character" better as "Hostile acts."

Claim
With object-noun means "lay claim to." Not to

105

be used as a substitute for declare, maintain, or charge.

Childish-Childlike

Childish refers to the unattractive features of children such as stubborness, temper tantrums, etc. Childlike refers to the best in children like sweetness, innocence, faith, etc.

Combat-Contest

Combat is a fight, a struggle between enemies. A contest may be merely a competition and may be between neutrals or friends.

Compare

To compare is to point out or imply resemblance between objects regarded as essentially of different order; to compare *with* is mainly to point out differences between objects regarded as essentially of the same order. (Paris has been compared to ancient Athens; it may be compared with modern London.)

Dependant-Dependent-Dependence

Dependant is a noun meaning "a person who depends on another for support, position, etc." Dependent, an adjective, means hanging down and "having its existence conditioned by that of something else." Dependence is the state of being dependant.

Dialect-Dialogue

Dialect is a variation of the standard language characteristic of groups of people or regions of a country: New England dialect. When you write down the actual conversation of people, you are writing dialogue.

Discover-Invent

To discover something is to find something that was there before you came upon it (Columbus discovered America). To invent something is to create something new (Eli Whitney invented the cotton gin).

Disinterested-Uninterested

Disinterested: aloof from
Uninterested: indifferent

Distinguish-Discriminate

Distinguish: differentiate
Discriminate: appreciate

Divided into

Not to be misused for composed of. A difficult line to draw: plays are divided into acts, but poems are composed of stanzas; an apple, halved, is divided into sections, but an apple is composed of seeds, flesh, and skin.

Divers-Diverse

Divers: various
Diverse: differing

Don't

Contraction of do not. The contraction of does not is doesn't.

Dual-Duel

Dual: belonging to two or shared by two
Duel: contest between two persons fought with deadly weapons

Empty-Vacant

Empty: containing nothing (a jug without water)
Vacant: a house or room that is unoccupied, in which there are no people

Enormity

Use only in the sense of monstrous wickedness. Misleading, if not wrong, when used to express bigness. The latter is enormousness.

Enquiry-Inquiry

An enquiry is a quest for a simple fact such as the time of a train.
An inquiry is an investigation.

Ensure-Insure-Assure

Ensure means to make certain. Insure is confined to life-insurance and similar contracts. Assure means giving one's word.

Etc.

Means and other things, and also now is used to mean and other persons. Do not use at end of a list introduced by such as, for example, or similar expressions.

Excuse-Pardon

Small slips are excused; more considerable faults (and crimes) are pardoned.

Evoke-Invoke

Evoke: obtain effect
Invoke: appeal for effect

Exceptional-Exceptionable

Exceptional: unusual
Exceptionable: objectionable

Fact

Use this word only of matters of a kind capable of direct verification, not of matters of judgment. That a particular event happened on a given date is a fact. That Napoleon was the greatest of modern generals is not.

Faker-Fakir

Faker: pretender
Fakir: mendicant

Famous-Notorious

Famous means well-known for something admirable, useful. Notorious means well-known but in an unfavorable light.

Farther-Further

The two words are commonly interchanged. However, farther serves best as a distance word, further as a time or quantity word.

Fewer-Less

Fewer refers to number. Less refers to amount or degree. (I am taking fewer subjects. This year we had less rainfall.)

Fix

Approved colloquial for arrange, prepare, mend. But it once referred only to the verb meaning to make firm, to place definitely. These still are preferred meanings.

Flowed-Flown

Learn verb parts for fly and flew. Fly: fly, flew, flown. Flow: flow, flowed, flowed. Don't say water has flown under the bridge (that's flying water).

Folk-Folks

Collective noun equivalent to people and used in singular form only. Folks, in the sense of parents, family, these present, is colloquial and too folksy usually for writing.

Fortuitously

This does not mean fortunately; it means by accident.

Generally-Commonly

Generally: for the most part
Commonly: usually

Get

Colloquial "have got" for "have" should not be used in writing. (Instead of: He has not got any sense. . .say: He has no sense.)

Good-Well

Good is usually an adjective and must modify or complete the meaning of a noun (His art work is good). Well is used both as adjective and adverb. It is an adjective only when it refers to health.

Hanged-Hung

Principal parts of hang when referring to the death penalty are hang, hanged, hanged. In other senses they are hang, hung, hung.

Healthful-Healthy-Wholesome

You are healthy. The things that promote good health are healthful. Wholesome refers to salubrious.

He is a man who

Common redundancy. Don't say: He is a man who is very ambitious. Say: He is very ambitious.

However

Avoid starting a sentence with however when the meaning is nevertheless. The word usually serves better when not in first position. (The roads were almost impassable. However, we at last succeeded in reaching camp. . . .The roads were almost impassable. At last, however, we succeeded in reaching camp.)

Human-Humane

Human means characteristic of man. Humane means tender, kind, compassionate.

Illegible-Ineligible

Poor handwriting can be illegible. Ineligible refers to a person's not having the necessary qualifications.

Illicit-Elicit

Illicit: unlawful
Elicit: draw out

Immigrate-Emigrate

Immigrate means to come into another country after leaving your native land. Emigrate means to leave your native land.

Immoral-Unmoral

Immoral: violates morals
Unmoral: without morals

Imply-Infer

Imply means to hint. Infer means to find out by reasoning, to draw a conclusion from facts.

Incredible-Incredulous

A story or situation is incredible (unbelievable); a person is incredulous (unbelieving).

Ingenious-Ingenuous

Ingenious means clever, skillful, resourceful, inventive. Ingenuous means, sincere, honest, open.

Intelligent-Intelligible

Intelligent means alert, wise. Intelligible means capable of being understood.

Involve-Implicate

Involve: involuntary entanglement
Implicate: voluntary entanglement

Inaugurate-Initiate-Begin

Inaugurate means to induct into office. Initiate means to make a member. Begin means to start.

Inside of-Inside

The of following inside is correct in the adverbial meaning "in less than." In other meanings the additional word is unnecessary.

Interesting

A weak word. Instead of announcing that what you are about to tell is interesting, just make it so.

In the last analysis

Cut it.

Irregardless

Should be regardless.

Kind of

Except in familiar style not to be used as a substitute for rather or something like.

Last-Latest

Last: the end
Latest: most recent

Lay-Lie

Lay means to put something down. Lay must always take an object. (Principal parts: I lay or am laying; I laid; I have laid). Lie means to recline (or to tell an untruth). (Principal parts: I lie or am lying; I lay; I have lain). One lays a book on the shelf, but one lies down on a bed.

Leave

Not to be misused for let. (Incorrect: Leave it stand the way it is. Correct: Let it stand the way it is.)

Like-As

Like governs nouns and pronouns; before phrases and clauses the equivalent word is as.

Literal-Literally

Often incorrectly used in support of exaggeration or violent metaphor. (Incorrect: A literal flood of abuse, or literally dead with fatigue. Correct: A flood of abuse, or almost dead with fatigue).

Loan-Lend

Lean: noun, never a verb
Lend: a verb

Locate-Settle
Locate: find or determine
Settle: rest or reside

Mad-Angry
Mad: insane
Angry: aroused ire

Most
Not to be used for almost.

Mutual-Common
Mutual: reciprocal
Common: shared

Nature
Often simply redundant. (Hostile acts is better than acts of a hostile nature.)

None
Takes a singular verb. This rule applies also to each, each one, everybody, everyone, many a man, nobody.

Nice-Agreeable
Nice: precise
Agreeable: pleasant

Notorious-Notable
Notorious: bad repute
Notable: distinguished

Novice-Amateur
Novice: beginner
Amateur: non-professional

Oftentimes, ofttimes
Archaic forms. Use "often."

One of the most
Feeble.

Oldest-Eldest
Oldest: most old
Eldest: specifically of persons

Out loud-Aloud
Out loud is vulgar.

People
Best not used with words of number, in place of persons.

Permit-Allow
Permit: formal consent
Allow: tacit consent

Persecute-Prosecute
Persecute means to annoy, to plague, to hunt down, to bring suffering. Prosecute means to carry out a legal action.

Personalize
A pretentious word. (Better to say "a highly personal affair" than "a highly personalized affair".)

Personally
Often unnecessary.

Perpetual-Continual
Perpetual: eternal
Continual: all along

Phase
Means a stage of transition or development. Not to be used for aspect or topic (another point rather than another phase of the subject).

Phenomenon-Phenomena
Phenomenon is singular; phenomena the plural.

Pour-Spill
When you pour a cup of tea, you fill the cup. When you spill a cup of tea, you accidentally upset the cup and the tea runs out.

Practical-Practicable
Practical: actually effective
Practicable: capable of being made effective

Precede-Proceed
Precede means to go before. Proceed means to go on or forward.

Principal-Principle
Principal: chief participant
Principle: doctrine

Protagonist

Originally the actor who played the principal part in a Greek drama. Not to be used for advocate or supporter.

Proven

Archaic for proved.

Real-Very

Real: actual
Very: extremely

Recollect-Remember

Recollect: revive in memory
Remember: to exercise memory

Respectfully-Respectively

Respectfully means showing respect or honor to someone. Respectively refers to a number of items taken in order.

Rout-Route

To rout means to defeat completely. A route is an overwhelming defeat. A route is a road. To route means to send by way of a certain road or route.

Revenge-Avenge

Revenge: punishment inflicted
Avenge: act of inflicting punishment

Satisfied-Convinced

Satisfied: fulfilled
Convinced: beyond doubt

Secure-Obtain

Secure: made safe
Obtain: get

Series

Not synonymous with group or collection. Members of a series—it is a singular noun—must have some feature that is common to them all. One refers to a series of articles run in a magazine, but not to a series of bladder cases (this is a collection).

Shall-Will

In formal writing, the future tense requires shall for the first person, will for the second and third. Also when the speaker expresses belief regarding his future action or state, he says: I shall. If he expresses his determination or his consent, he says: I will.

Sit-Set

Set is to place or put. Sit is what you do to yourself.

So

Avoid as an intensifier: like so good, so warm, so delightful.

Split Infinitive

Avoid when possible. Make it "to inquire diligently" rather than "to diligently inquire."

Similate-Simulate

Similate: to be like
Simulate: to pretend

Staid-Stayed

Staid: sober, sedate
Stayed: remained

Stationary-Stationery

Stationary means remaining in one place. Stationery means writing paper, envelopes, etc.

Status

This means position in society or a profession. It does not refer to state or condition.

Stop-Stay

Stop: cease
Stay: remain

Sustained-Suffered

Sustained: upheld
Suffered: as suffered a wound

The Foreseeable Future

A fuzzy cliche.

Tortuous-Torturous

A winding road is tortuous; a painful ordeal is torturous.

Transpire-Occur
Transpire: to become known
Occur: happen

Type
Not a synonym for kind of.

Understand-Know
Understand: to grasp
Know: to be aware of

Uninterested-Disinterested
Uninterested means not interested. A disinterested person is one who has no desire to gain something for himself.

Unique
Means being without a like or equal. There can be no degrees of uniqueness.

Ugly-Nasty
Ugly: repulsive
Nasty: disagreeable

Verbal-Oral
Verbal: written or spoken
Oral: spoken only

Very
Use this word sparingly.

Want-Wish
Want: acute need
Wish: desire

While
Avoid the indiscriminate use of this word for and, but, and although.